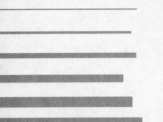

CONTINENT OF EXTREMES

The strange, as it were, invisible beauty of Australia, which is undeniably there, but which seems to lurk just beyond the range of our white vision. You feel you can't see it—as if your eyes hadn't the vision in them to correspond with the outside landscape. For the landscape is so unimpressive … it hangs back so aloof. And yet, when you don't have the feeling of ugliness or monotony … you get a sense of subtle, remote, formless beauty more poignant that anything ever experienced before …

D.H. LAWRENCE, *Kangaroo*

D1377476

Cover photograph
Southern wall of Kings Canyon, George Gill Range, Northern Territory.

Inside front cover

Top left: Fitzroy Falls, Southern Tablelands of New South Wales, are 183 m high (in two drops).

Top right: Magnetic termite mounds, Litchfield National Park, Northern Territory. Termite mounds, located on an alluvial plain, are aligned north-south to minimise the effects of solar heating.

Centre left: The Bubbler Mound Spring, a natural outlet of the Great Artesian Basin, near Lake Eyre South, South Australia.

Centre right: Summit area of Mt Kosciuszko in the Snowy Mountains, New South Wales. This is continental Australia's highest point.

Bottom left: Katherine Gorge in the Northern Territory, at 60 m deep is not one of the deepest gorges in Australia but it is one of the most spectacular.

Bottom right: Kata Tjuta (Mt Olga), west of Uluru, Northern Territory, with Olga Gorge (the deepest gorge in the Northern Territory) on the right. The giant monoliths are some 65 square kilometres in area.

Inside back cover

Top left: Atila (Mt Conner), east of Uluru, Northern Territory, is a remnant plateau formation rising above a sandplain. A small saltlake can be seen in the middle distance.

Top right: Port Campbell coastline, Western Districts, Victoria, is part of Victoria's longest cliffline.

Centre left: South Molle Island, off Queensland coast. Behind the island lies the Whitsundays Passage, which at 70 km long, is one of the longest passages in Australia.

Centre right: Jump-up (low flat-top hills) country near Betoota, Channel Country, Queensland, is a stony or gibber desert.

Bottom left: The Trans-continental railway line is the longest straight railway in the world on a vast rocky plain. One of the stops along the line is Cook Siding on the Nullarbor Plain, South Australia.

Bottom right: Longitudinal dune crest near Old Andado Station, Simpson Desert, Northern Territory. Mobile and oscillating dune crests such as this one are subject to movement by winds.

Other books by the author

The Bush: A Guide to the Vegetated Landscapes of Australia
Australia's Eastern Outback: The Driving Guide
Australia's Central and Western Outback: The Driving Guide
Australia's Northern Outback: The Driving Guide
Australia's Wet Tropics and North-Eastern Outback: The Driving Guide

A UNSW Press book

Published by
UNIVERSITY OF NEW SOUTH WALES PRESS LTD
University of New South Wales
Sydney 2052 Australia

© I.G. Read
First published in 1998

This book is copyright. Apart from any fair dealing for the purpose of private study, research, criticism or review, as permitted under the Copyright Act, no part may be reproduced by any process without written permission. Inquiries should be addressed to the publisher.

National Library of Australia
Cataloguing-in-Publication entry:

Read, Ian G.
 Continent of Extremes: Recording Australia's Natural Phenomena

 Bibliography.
 Includes index.
 ISBN 0 86840 624 4.

 1. Australia—Geography. I. Title.

919.4

A catalogue record for this book is available from the Library of Congress, Washington, DC, USA. Library of Congress Catalog Card Number: 98-60218.

Cover design Di Quick
Text design Dana Lundmark
Printer Griffin Press

All photographs are by the author.

Disclaimer: While every attempt has been made to ensure the accuracy of the information contained in this book, things change over time and some of the extremes listed may well be exceeded during the lifetime of this book.

CONTINENT OF EXTREMES

RECORDING AUSTRALIA'S NATURAL PHENOMENA

Ian G. Read

UNSW PRESS

Symbols and Abbreviations

The locations of many of the features described in this book are shown on maps 1 to 9.

°	degrees
'	minutes
°C	degrees Celsius
°F	degrees Fahrenheit
approx.	approximate
BP	Before the Present
ca	*circa* (about)
E	east
ft	feet
ha	hectares
HS	homestead
Hwy	highway
km	kilometres
km^2	square kilometres
km/hr	kilometres per hour
m	metres
m/hr	metres per hour
mm	millimetres
n.a.	not available
OSA	Off-shore Australia
S	south
Stn	station

CONTENTS

ILLUSTRATIONS

Maps

Figures

TABLES

Chapter 1

Chapter 2

Chapter 3

Chapter 4

Chapter 5

Chapter 6

Chapter 7

Chapter 8

ACKNOWLEDGMENTS

The compilation of this work would not have been possible without the assistance of many organisations. Although the information in the book has been kept up to date, initial research began during the 1980s. Many of the organisations listed below no longer exist under their old names. In order to credit the people who worked within those organisation I have included the names of those organisations when the help was provided. To these individuals, too many to name, thank you.

Access Community Training, Corrimal, New South Wales
Australian Conservation Foundation
Australian National Railways Commission (Tasmania)
Country Roads Board, Victoria
Dept of the Capital Territory
Dept of Chief Minister, Northern Territory Information Service
Dept of Lands, Northern Territory
Dept of Lands, Western Australia
Dept of Main Roads, Tasmania
Dept of Science, Bureau of Meteorology
Dept of Transport and Works, Northern Territory
Highways Dept, South Australia
Katoomba Scenic Railway and Skyway
Land Administration Commission, Dept of Lands, Queensland
Main Roads Dept, Queensland
Main Roads Dept, Western Australia
Mapping Staff, State Library of Victoria
Ministry of Transport, Victoria
National Capital Development Commission
National Parks and Wildlife Service, New South Wales
National Parks and Wildlife Service, Tasmania
National Parks Service, Victoria
Nomenclature Advisory Committee, Dept of Lands, Western Australia
Perisher Blue
Premier's Dept, Queensland
Queensland Railways
Roads and Traffic Authority, Sydney
State Government Information and Inquiry Centre, Western Australia
State Library of Queensland
State Rail Authority of New South Wales
Survey and Mapping Division, Dept of Lands, Northern Territory
Surveyor-General's Office, Dept of Crown Lands and Survey, Victoria
VicRoads
Western Australia Government Railways
Westrail

I would also like to thank Coralyn Treasure for her critical comments, general assistance, proofreading abilities, and for assisting in the typing of many drafts, and the compilation and organisation of copies of the tables. Her help was immeasurable. Also many thanks to Susan Jorgensen for her critical appraisal, proofreading and comments. Thanks also to Geoff Cater and Lesley Speed for use of their printer. Finally, many thanks to Patsy Graham for typing the early drafts. Her assistance was greatly appreciated.

Ian G. Read

PERCEPTIONS OF THE LAND

ABORIGINAL PERCEPTIONS

> Aborigines believe that, in the beginning there were floods, then a great void, then the creating beings woke out of a deep sleep. These creating beings, the kangaroo, caterpillar, penguin and so on, travelled a special path—creating along the way—then settled down in some ossified form, a river, a mountain, waterfalls, a flow of bushes. These forms are the sacred sites. They are not dead, but still living. Each Aborigine relates to one particular creative being and its sacred site is the on-going force of his life today.
>
> Father Dobson, *Age* 1981

Australia has been occupied by Aborigines for a very long time. All of the continent has been occupied by them, including parts of its undersea margins during times of lower sea levels. Their basic unit of occupation, as described by non-Aborigines, was the 'tribe', but perhaps a better term is 'clan group', as the word 'tribe' suggests strict boundaries. A clan group is drawn together by some common identity. It is a group of people related by mythical and real connections to a piece of country over which they had exclusive rights to exist by hunting, fishing and gathering and by the practice of rituals. The hunting, fishing and gathering took place on land known as the 'economic range', and rituals were carried out on the 'ritual estate': these two tracts of country were not, however, necessarily the same.

At different times various clan groups would congregate for festivals and feasts; other gatherings would occur for trade or ceremonial purposes. Trade crossed clan group ranges and was a means of obtaining goods that were locally unavailable or in short supply. Ceremonies, customs and myths were also transferred across these ranges with the result that similar practices and beliefs are shared between neighbouring clan groups— across Australia. Although from neighbouring clan group to clan group variations were locally generally slight, greater variations existed between clan groups continent-wide. Nevertheless, Aborigines across Australia had common creation beliefs.

Clan groups varied in number from well below 100 people to as many as 400–500, and the size of each group's economic range basically depended on its available food supply. This, in turn, was dependent on rainfall; it is thought that in arid regions clan groups required about 50,000 km^2 of land and in areas of moderately high rainfall, about 5000 km^2. Described as nomadic, Aborigines moved systematically through their lands, going to particular areas at particular seasons according to where and when there would be a plentiful supply of food and water. As they travelled, the Aborigines would visit special places, perform rituals and celebrate ceremonies. They were intimately familiar with their land.

It used to be thought that the Aborigines did not husband and farm the land—in the way Europeans did—and that, therefore, the land was unoccupied. The land was considered to be *terra nullius*, which means 'a land belonging to nobody'. Because the land appeared not to be farmed, because animals appeared not to be husbanded, because the land appeared not to be owned by anyone, the European occupiers took the land and used it for their own ends without due regard or consideration for the Aborigines and certainly without compensation. But cultural prejudice is blind: the new occupants of the land could not see the effects of the 'firestick farming' carried out by their predecessors; they were ignorant of responsibilities different people had for their particular tracts of land. They were also blind, or indifferent, to the flourishing culture that had survived at least two thousand generations of occupation—the world's oldest.

Aborigines had, and many still do have a profound relationship to their land. Basic to their beliefs is the idea that they share the same life-force with all the elements of the landscape and all the natural species within it. Such a concept underpins all human faith—something that many non-Aborigines are once more realising. For the Aborigines this view of the life-force is expressed through their concept of the Dreaming.

Aborigines believe that during the Dreaming ancestral beings with supernatural power and energy traversed the Earth and, as they travelled, formed the topography of the land. They believe that the energies of these ancestral beings remain embodied within the earth along the tracks they followed and at special places where particular events took place. Not too much attention should be given to the ancestral beings themselves. Although they are said to shape the land, they have actually humanised it, making the land relevant to human living.

The places where the beings stopped are the sacred sites. Such sacred sites include hills, rocks, trees, waterholes, and many other natural objects. The significance of the sites is that part of the spiritual substance of life is contained there, so that as Aborigines move through the landscape, the landscape would reveal signs of this spiritual substance. A sacred site is difficult to define, for the energies it contains gradually diminish away from its centre. Hence, there is no definite boundary or cut-off point by which a sacred place can be specifically delineated (this concept has parallels with the ideas of energy fields in physics).

The term 'sacred sites' has crept into the Australian consciousness and language as Aborigines have become politicised. Opponents of land rights for Aborigines have claimed that sacred sites are invented wherever a miner or other interested party attempts to claim what the Aborigines responsible for that piece of country see as theirs. But sacred sites are just one type of site. They have not been invented for some political purpose; they have always been there. It is just that they come to light when there is conflict for land.

There are many named sites in the Aboriginal landscape. Some are related to plants, animals or natural phenomena such as wind or lightning: these are called totemic sites, and may or may not be 'sacred' (in a non-Aboriginal sense). Other sites relate to the supply of food (plants and animals) and resources (stones, timber, bark, medicine, tobacco, and so on), the distribution of which controls the traditional patterns of movement. These are called capital sites; their location, or proximity to each other, dictates how the land is utilised. Among other sites are those used for ceremonies and rituals, many of which are both sacred and secret. Other sites are used when times are tough, or during inter-clan group celebrations and feasts. There are sites where rock art occurs, usually in association with rituals and ceremonies, and there are named and unnamed sites which may simply be of historical interest or be highly significant in Aboriginal traditional narratives.

Aborigines gained their energy (their purpose of living) from these sacred sites, from the Dreamtime tracks, and from the land in between. This is proudly proclaimed as 'my country'—a concept common among non-Aborigines, too, for example as an affinity for land through childhood associations, through succeeding generations of occupation, or through familiar or cherished memories. Each thing held so dear is an enrichment of life, a connection between a person and the forces of life contained within that special place.

Responsibility for conserving the land passes down from generation to generation within Aboriginal clan groups. How these clans are arranged, and their associated kinship ties, is a complex matter and varies from place to place but it is sufficient to say that those who have the knowledge—gained through initiation ceremonies, and so on—become the 'caretakers' of the land. This is a spiritual connection that exists, by virtue of his or her birth, between an individual caretaker and a site or area of country. It is not 'ownership', in the non-Aboriginal sense, for Aborigines perceive the land to be a part of themselves and themselves to be a part of the land.

This connection between the caretakers, the land and the Dreamtime is maintained by ceremonies performed by the clan. Through the ceremonies the Dreamtime energies are kept alive, and the knowledge is passed on to successive generations. Past, present and future is regarded as an uninterrupted cycle. The spirit of the Dreaming, being brought to life by the birth of children, is passed on to the people, the land and all it contains through various rituals. As it is the source of all life, everything the Dreaming touches is sacred, and sacredness becomes a part of living. Initiation practices reinforce the Aborigine to the sacred. Death is another form of initiation, which returns the spirit to the Dreaming; this, turning full circle, once again creates life from death.

Obviously, the land is important to the Aborigines. But if it is taken away from them—if they become dispossessed, it means that the ceremonies break down. The result is that energies are reduced; the life-force is lost and, consequently, so too is the Aborigines' identity. In its place are the ills of all dispossessed people: ill-health, drunkenness, violence, and so on. For the Australian Aborigines, to lose the land is to lose themselves.

TABLE 1.1
FIRST CONTACTS BETWEEN ABORIGINES AND EUROPEANS

DATE	CLAN GROUP	REGION
1630s	Tiwi	Melville-Bathurst Islands
1640s	Gagudju	Top End, Northern Territory
1770s	Eora	Sydney
1770s	Banjelang	New South Wales north coast
1830s	Ngarrindjeri	Murray River, South Australia
1830s	Barkinji	Western Plains, New South Wales
1840s	Kurnai	Gippsland, Victoria
1840s	Dieri	Cooper Creek, South Australia
1860s	Arrernte	Central Australia
1860s	Mitakoodi	north-western Queensland
1860s	Kalkadoons	north-western Queensland
1870s	Pitjantjatjara	Western Desert
1870s	Walpiri	Tanami Desert
1890s	Pintupi	Great Sandy Desert

The dates in table 1.1 are approximate and indicate the time of likely first contact between Aboriginal groups and Europeans; coastal Ngarrindjeri and Kurnai people probably had earlier contact with Europeans. It is possible that most groups would have had some knowledge of the Europeans before first contact. Contact was not immediately followed by occupation and settlement, particularly in the desert areas, although once the pastoral and agricultural frontier pushed further inland Aboriginal groups faced major disruptions to their lives and, in most cases, loss of their land. Of the groups listed in this table only the Gagudju, Pitjantjatjara, Walpiri and Pintupi people maintained their traditional way of life well into the 20th century.

Some 'first contacts' have occurred in the recent past. The Pintupi, along with the Wangkatja people of the Great Victoria Desert, were the last large groups to be 'brought in' during the clearance of the Woomera Rocket Range in the 1950s and early 1960s. In the late 1960s and early 1970s there were still a number of Budidjara, Gadudjara, Ngdadjara and Wanman people living traditionally in the western arid regions. By the mid 1970s the traditional lands of these peoples were virtually empty for the first time in possibly 30,000 years. Following this, in 1977, the last two Mandildjara people of the Gibson Desert, Western Australia, were encouraged to join their kinsfolk in the settled districts.

In October 1984 a small group was contacted in the Stansmore Range area of the Great Sandy Desert, Western Australia. Although at the time this was thought to be a first contact, it seems likely that they knew about life in the outside world. The last contact was in 1986 when seven Wangkatja people decided to join their kin at an Aboriginal settlement on the edge of the Great Victoria Desert, Western Australia. In my own travels during the late 1980s I have met some Western Desert Aborigines who believed that there were still some small groups living traditionally in those parts. Interestingly, my informants described themselves as 'going to Australia' when leaving their traditional country for the settled districts. Of course, with the granting of land rights, coupled with the homeland or outstation movement, many semi-traditional Aborigines are returning to their own country.

EXPLORATION AND DISCOVERY

Until recently it was thought that Aborigines arrived in Australia between 40,000 and 60,000 years before the present (BP). Recent archaeological discoveries in the Jinmium area of the Keep River district, Northern Territory, have unearthed stone tools which some researchers believe date back 170,000 years. If they are this old, the question is whether these tools were used by the ancestors of modern Aborigines or by archaic hominids. More recent studies have cast considerable doubt on the age of these tools, with some researchers dating them at around 12,000 years old. Nonetheless, the Aboriginal presence can be confidently dated back approximately 60,000 years.

None of the early explorers happened upon the more benign east coast of Australia until Cook, although some people believe that the Portuguese may have travelled along Australia's southern and eastern coasts. One piece of inconclusive evidence supports this theory: the supposed remains of a 'mahogany ship' which may have been Portuguese in origin. Last seen in the 1880s, it is now deeply buried in sand dunes west of Warrnambool, Victoria.

Further support for the theory that Australia was known to the Portuguese comes from an early map known as the Dauphin Chart, published *ca* 1536. On this map was depicted a landmass bearing some similarity to Australia, which was called Java la

Grande. It is not beyond the realms of possibility that the Portuguese visited Australia, and that Mendonca may have explored its coastline. The Portuguese settlement in Timor was only some 500 kilometres off the northern Australian coast. Various maps were published in succeeding years, among them the Frobisher map of 1578 and the Wytfliet map of 1597, in both of which Australia was called Terra Australis. But it was Jansz's visit in the *Duyfken* in 1606 that was the earliest known European contact with Australia.

Any European exploration of Australia may, however, have been preceded by the Chinese. From 1405 to 1453 the Chinese navigator Cheng Ho made several voyages south to the Timor area and could have made contact with Australia. The scant evidence for this includes a Chinese soapstone carving dating from the 1400s, which was found near Darwin, and a piece of porcelain located in the Gulf of Carpentaria region. Given that the Chinese had visited the east African coast, a voyage to Australian shores is not unrealistic. Other Asian contacts include the Bajo fishermen (known as sea nomads, and currently based on Roti Island, Indonesia), who have been fishing around Ashmore Island for over 400 years, as evidenced by groves of coconuts, garden remains and graves.

In 1606 the explorer de Quiros thought he had discovered the southern continent when he found what in fact was one of the islands of Vanuatu, which he named La Austrialia del Espíritu Santo. In *circa* 1628 a Dutch map referred to Australia as Terra del Zur (literally, Land of the South) and a later Dutch map, the Janssonius map of 1657, was one of the first to show the western Australian coastline virtually complete from Cape York to the Nullarbor Plain as well as parts of Van Diemen's Land. Australia was then referred to as Hollandia Nova, or New Holland.

In 1770 the eastern half of the Australian continent was claimed by the Englishman, Captain Cook, who, it is alleged, named it New South Wales. In fact, it was the ghost-writer of his journals, Dr Hawkesworth, who originated this name. Nowhere in Cook's or his officers' original papers does the name New South Wales occur.

By the time the first settlement was established at Sydney Cove in 1788 most of the Australian coastline was known to the Europeans, the exception being parts of the south and south-east. Bass, in his open whaleboat, sailed the Gippsland coast to Western Port in 1798. In the same year Flinders sailed amongst the Furneaux Group of islands, off Tasmania's north-east coast. Both men concluded that Van Diemen's Land was an island and, together, circumnavigated it in 1798–99. Grant sailed through Bass Strait along the Victorian coast in 1800. The French navigator Baudin sailed westwards along the Victorian and South Australian coasts in 1801, meeting Flinders at Encounter Bay. Flinders was heading east after having explored the coast between Nuytsland and Encounter Bay, including the Spencer and St Vincent gulfs. Murray filled in a gap by exploring Port Phillip Bay in 1802.

In 1805 Flinders championed the name Australia, which appeared on his 1814 map, the 'General Chart of Terra Australis or Australia'. Governor Macquarie was the first to officially use the name Australia, on a document in 1817.

TABLE 1.2
EXPLORATION AND DISCOVERY OF THE AUSTRALIAN LANDMASS: BEFORE 1788

DATE	EXPLORER(S)	LOCATION EXPLORED/DISCOVERED
170,000 BP	Aborigines/archaic hominids	via Australian northern coast
60,000 BP	Aborigines	via Australian northern coast
?	Melanesians	Torres Strait Islands
?	Malays (?)	Australian northern coast
AD 1400s	Cheng Ho (?)	?Australian northern coast
AD 1521	Mendonca (?)	?Java la Grande (?Australian east coast)
1530 ca	Portuguese explorers (?)	?Java la Grande (?north-west coast of Western Australia)
1600 ca	Bajo fishermen	Ashmore Island and Arnhem Land
1606	Jansz	Cape Keerweer and Gulf of Carpentaria
1606	Torres	Torres Strait
1616	Hartog	Dirk Hartog Island (Shark Bay, Western Australia)
1619	Edels	Edelsland (north-western Western Australia)
1622	Gerritsz	Cape Leeuwin (south-western Western Australia)
1623	Carstensz	Arnhem Land
1627	Nuyts	Nuytsland (Nullarbor cliffs, Western Australia)
1628	Wits	Witsland (Pilbara region)
1629	Pelsaert	Houtman Abrolhos
1636	Pieterszoon	Van Diemen's Land and Melville Island
1642	Tasman	Van Diemen's Land (southern Tasmania)
1644	Tasman	Gulf of Carpentaria to Pilbara
1688	Dampier	Dampier Land (Kimberley region)
1697	de Vlamingh	Dirk Hartog Island and Vlamingh Head (Shark Bay and Exmouth Peninsula, Western Australia)
1699	Dampier	Shark Bay, Western Australia
1700 ca	Macassan voyagers	Marege (Anhem Land, northern coast-line)
1770	Cook	New Holland (Australian east coast)
1777	Furneaux	Van Diemen's Land (north-eastern Tasmania)

NON-ABORIGINAL PERCEPTIONS

Many non-Aboriginal people have seen the Australian landscape as an unfriendly place. With the growth and spread of European occupation during the 19th century and early 20th century, most settlers were concerned with wresting a living from what they saw as a hostile environment. The European settlers came from lands that were closely settled and green, and had weather that was generally cool and moist—even if in their immediate past some were more accustomed to the impoverished dwellings and habitats of industrial society.

Despite Australia being hotter and drier than Europe, it was optimistically thought that settlement would push back the margins of the desert—an idea that faded only one or two generations ago.

> The soils of the plains are loose, and in very dry weather the grass nearly disappears; but as the country becomes stocked and the tread of the animals binds the surface; the grass acquires closeness and strength and the saltbush gives way to the characteristics of the [Western] slopes [of New South Wales]. As a consequence the rain that falls begins to form watercourses, watercourses become creeks and the streams increase in volume.
>
> G.H. Reid, 1874 (who later became prime minister of Australia, 1904–05)

In fact, the opposite occurred to what Reid predicted. The animals' tread compacted the soil and the rain ran over the surface, eroding it and infilling the creeks and waterholes with sediment. The plentiful rains of a few successive years that led people further and further towards the margins of the desert were aberrations. Dry seasons followed with crop failures and sheep deaths. With practices such as the overstocking of sheep on the western plains of New South Wales and the advancing cropping frontier of South Australia, the soil became compacted and the vegetation was removed so that the topsoil lost its natural protective covering and became prone to wind erosion. The hot north-westerlies of spring carried the, by then powdery dust into Adelaide, Melbourne or across the Tasman Sea to New Zealand. Dust storms became an Australian climatic feature. Instead of being pushed back, the desert itself pushed towards the settled districts: the desertification of Australia had begun. Even today the erosion scars and depleted range-lands wrought by these activities are still evident.

The European settlers had little or no experience of climatic fluctuations, particularly rainfall. Believing that 'rain would follow the plough', they marched off into marginal country during the (unknown to them) good seasons. It is sad to reflect that, even though we know better today, from time to time various governments and organisations still would like to expand the cropping frontier further and further into the dry country. Not so long ago it was proposed that the land be partially cleared to the Darling River in New South Wales; that the South Yilgarn and Dundas Wilderness areas in Western Australia be turned over to wheat cropping; that broadacre cotton farms be established, based on irrigation from the widely fluctuating seasonal river flows of Cooper Creek in western Queensland. These areas are considered marginal: that is, they are only capable of producing crops now and then, owing to low and unreliable rainfall. While politicians and developers blather on about new technologies making the land more productive, who can forget that final dramatic scene at the end of the 1979–83 drought when top-soil from the marginal, already established Mallee wheatlands was dumped by a giant dust storm on Melbourne, reducing visibility to less than 100m.

What this tells us about non-Aboriginal Australians and their approach to the land is that they are still learning about the country; they are still seeking knowledge that will help them be productive, but not at the cost of environmental degradation. Behind the walls and facades of European occupation, there lies within Australia a hidden quality—a body of knowledge that is waiting to be tapped. This knowledge might enable those non-Aboriginal Australians to reach an understanding of this, their adopted country. This knowledge lies beyond physical power, intellectual knowledge or bureaucratic organisation. It embodies spirit and emotion—elements of our being that we, as products of a Westernised culture, have yet to realise or appreciate in terms of our understanding of our place within the world and its different environments.

Within the lore and culture of many Australian Aborigines there is knowledge about land and environment, and the deepest part of ourselves. To counter the greed and environmental degradation that has accompanied economic progress and adversely affected virtually every environment and landscape within Australia, our salvation may well come from those we, as a society, sought to subjugate. This resource is waiting to be tapped. Perhaps all we need to do is acknowledge the sins of our forebears—to seek reconciliation, be patient, and ask.

Early settlement

TABLE 1.3
FIRST TEMPORARY EUROPEAN SETTLEMENT IN EACH STATE/TERRITORY

NSW	(see below)	
Vic.	Sullivans Bay convict camp, Mornington Peninsula	1803
Qld	Redcliffe camp, Moreton Bay	1824
SA	Reeves Point (Kingscote), Kangaroo Island	1836
WA	Houtman Abrolhos islands	1629
Tas.	Risdon Cove, near Hobart	1803
NT	Fort Dundas, Melville Island	1824
ACT	Limestone Plains (Ginninderra)	1826

As a first settlement for New South Wales, it has been suggested that the ruins of a settlement at Bittangabee Inlet, on the south coast, predate Captain Cook and might be of Portuguese origin. Studies indicate, however, that it was probably an outstation established in the 1840s by Ben Boyd, of Boydtown fame.

In Victoria scant evidence remains of the Sullivans Bay camp, with some references stating that the convict camp at Western Port Bay, established in 1826, is the oldest European settlement. Also in Victoria there is the remains of a large stone village constructed by Aborigines near Lake Condah, Western Districts. In one area there are the ruined walls of up to 175 dwellings, capable of housing up to 1000 people. The site is about 2000–3000 years old.

In Queensland non-European settlements have existed on the Torres Strait islands for hundreds of years. Reference should also be made to Captain Cook's lay-over in 1770 on the Endeavour River at Cooktown. A temporary camp was established while he had his damaged ship repaired after it struck a coral reef.

In South Australia it is likely that sealers' or whalers' camps predate the Reeves Point settlement mentioned in table 1.3. The temporary settlement mentioned in this table for Western Australia was that of the survivors of the *Batavia* wreck, who lived on the Houtman Abrolhos islands and built fortifications there.

In the Northern Territory there are the remains of temporary settlements established by the Macassans in the 18th century.

THE OLDEST CONTINUALLY INHABITED PLACE IN AUSTRALIA IS AT MALANGANGERR IN THE KAKADU NATIONAL PARK, NORTHERN TERRITORY. UNTIL THE 1970S IT HAD BEEN OCCUPIED FOR 23,000 YEARS.

TABLE 1.4
OLDEST PERMANENT EUROPEAN SETTLEMENT IN EACH STATE/TERRITORY

NSW	Sydney Town	1788
Vic.	Portland	1834
Qld	Brisbane	1824
SA	Adelaide	1836
WA	Albany	1826
Tas.	Hobart Town	1803
NT	Palmerston (Darwin)	1868
ACT	Tharwa	1862
OSA	Norfolk Island	1788

```
┌───────────────────────────────────────────────────────────┐
│                        TABLE 1.5                            │
│          OLDEST EUROPEAN SETTLEMENTS IN AUSTRALIA           │
│                                                             │
│       1788              Sydney, NSW                         │
│       1788              Norfolk Island                      │
│       1790              Parramatta, NSW                     │
│       1803              Hobart Town, Tas.                   │
│       1804              Newcastle, NSW                      │
│       1804              Launceston, Tas.                    │
│       1807              New Norfolk, Tas.                   │
│       1810              Liverpool, NSW                      │
│       1810              The Macquarie Towns, NSW            │
└───────────────────────────────────────────────────────────┘
```

The dates in tables 1.4 and 1.5 are the respective years of establishment for each settlement. Tasmania at this time was, of course, known as Van Diemen's Land. The Macquarie Towns included Pitt Town, Windsor, Wilberforce, Castlereagh and Richmond. Bathurst, on the Central Tablelands of New South Wales, which is considered to be Australia's first inland town, was established in 1815.

By way of interest, the oldest known evidence of British colonisation is the initials and date 'FM 1788' (sounds like a radio station!) carved in sandstone rock at Garden Island, Sydney, by Frederick Merrideth from the First Fleet ship, the *Sirius*.

AUSTRALIA AT LARGE

Australia is a large island situated in the southern hemisphere between the Indian Ocean and Pacific Ocean basins. It is a continental landmass whose margins are submerged in relatively shallow waters. The underwater region between the coast and the continental margins is known as the continental shelf. This shelf forms seas, gulfs, bights and straits in some places—for example, the Arafura Sea, Gulf of Carpentaria, Great Australian Bight, Torres Strait. Off the north-eastern coast it also forms extensive barrier reefs, collectively known as the Great Barrier Reef. The most obvious feature of Australia is that it is a flat and low continent; vast plains cover much of its area. Even the uplands are relatively low tablelands and plateaus, and there are no major mountain ranges.

Australia has many ancient geological formations that have been preserved and the land has the appearance of being vast and old.

A STRING OF LOW MOUNTAINS, PLATEAUS AND HILLS, THE GREAT DIVIDING RANGE CONSTITUTES ONE OF THE LONGEST CONTINENTAL DIVIDES IN THE WORLD.

Gondwana legacy

From a comparison of fossil evidence and the shapes of continents at the undersea margins it is now assumed that all continents were once joined together. Combined with present-day South America, Africa, India, Antarctica, New Guinea and New Zealand, Australia was once a part of the ancient continent of Gondwana.

Australia was still connected with India and Antarctica 150 million years ago when dinosaurs roamed the land. Fossil footprints of dinosaurs can be seen today at Larks Quarry, south-west of Winton, Queensland. As India drifted towards Asia and the Tasman Sea was beginning to open out, shallow seas covered much of the Australian landmass, including the Cretaceous seas that were to become the Great Artesian Basin. Around this time flowering plants appeared. Following the separation of Australia from Antarctica there was considerable volcanic action along the Australian eastern seaboard and shallow seas covered today's Nullarbor Plain and the Murray Mallee.

Around 55 million years ago Australia's distinctive flora and fauna were evolving independently of the rest of the world. The distinctive shape of Australia's coastline would have been fairly recognisable for the last 50 million years, at least at the edge of the continental shelf. Because so little mountain building has occurred since the breakup of Gondwana, Australia has the relatively flat and low-lying landscape we see today.

Over the last one million years geological activity has continually taken place. Climates have changed, and sea levels rose and fell as ice ages came and went. At the last significant lowering of the sea level the Australian mainland was joined with Tasmania and New Guinea, and glaciers covered the high mountains of Tasmania. Minor glaciation also occurred on the high peaks around Mt Kosciuszko. There has been extensive volcanic activity relatively recently, resulting in basalt or lava flows in western Victoria and in northern Queensland. Australia's familiar coastline appeared about 6000 years ago, with sea levels then being roughly what they are today. Continental drift has continued throughout this period: Australia is steadily becoming a part of Asia, moving towards it at just less than 5 cm a year.

AUSTRALIA'S OLDEST LAND SURFACE, FOUND IN THE DAVENPORT RANGES NEAR THE DEVILS MARBLES, NORTHERN TERRITORY, IS ESTIMATED TO BE 500 MILLION YEARS OLD. THE OLDEST ROCK CRYSTALS IN AUSTRALIA, FOUND IN THE JACK HILLS, MURCHISON GOLDFIELDS, WESTERN AUSTRALIA, HAVE BEEN DATED AT 4300 MILLION YEARS OLD. IN THE SAME REGION ZIRCON MINERALS 4100 MILLION YEARS OLD HAVE BEEN FOUND IN ROCKS AT MT NARRYER. ALSO FROM THE SAME STATE ARE AUSTRALIA'S OLDEST FOSSILS: THESE ARE OF STROMATOLITES, DISCOVERED AT NORTH POLE WELL IN THE PILBARA, AND ARE APPROXIMATELY 3500 MILLION YEARS OLD.

Australia's physical extent

TABLE 2.1 LAND AREAS	
NSW	801,600 km^2
Vic.	227,600 km^2
Qld	1,727,200 km^2
SA	984,000 km^2
WA	2,525,500 km^2
Tas.	67,800 km^2
NT	1,346,200 km^2
ACT	2,400 km^2
AUSTRALIA	7,682,300 km^2

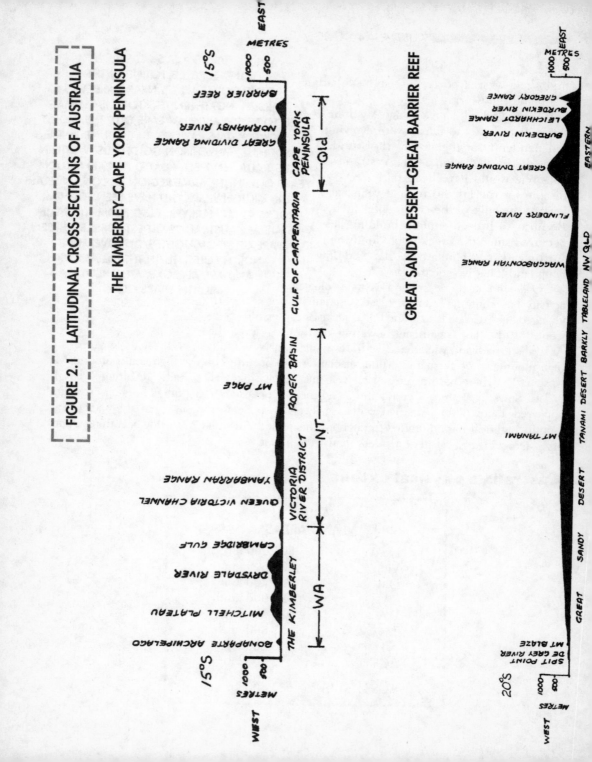

FIGURE 2.1 LATITUDINAL CROSS-SECTIONS OF AUSTRALIA

THE KIMBERLEY–CAPE YORK PENINSULA

GREAT SANDY DESERT–GREAT BARRIER REEF

GASCOYNE–FRASER ISLAND

BATAVIA COAST–GREAT DIVIDING RANGE

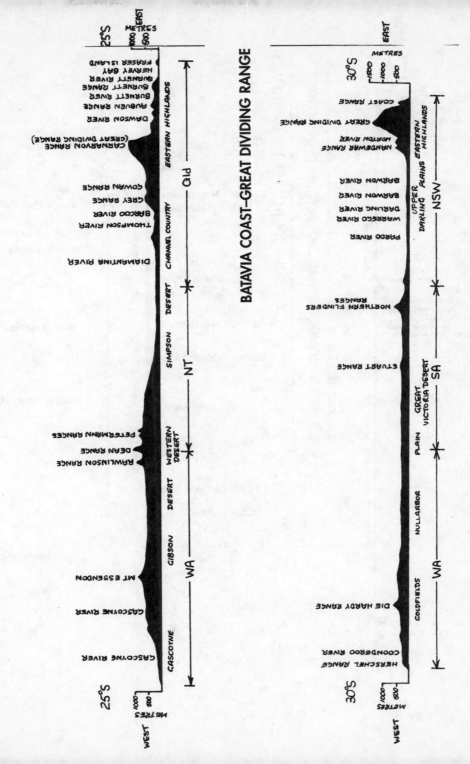

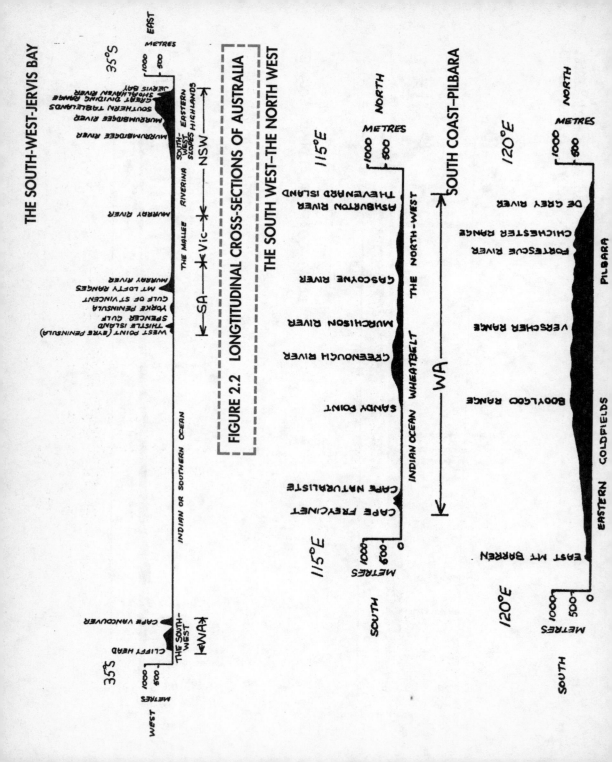

THE SOUTH-WEST–JERVIS BAY

FIGURE 2.2   LONGTITUDINAL CROSS-SECTIONS OF AUSTRALIA

THE SOUTH WEST–THE NORTH WEST

SOUTH COAST–PILBARA

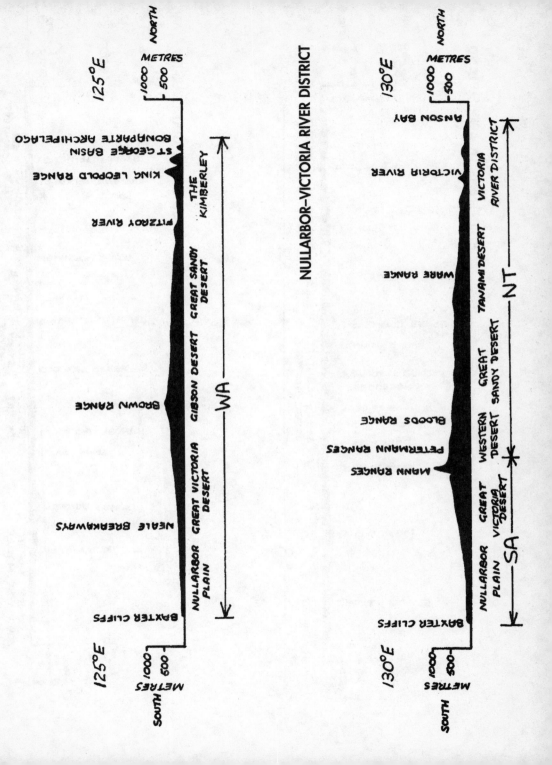

NULLARBOR—THE KIMBERLEY

125°E

NORTH

METRES
1000
500

BONAPARTE ARCHIPELAGO
ST GEORGE BASIN
KING LEOPOLD RANGE
THE KIMBERLEY

FITZROY RIVER

GREAT SANDY DESERT

GIBSON DESERT

BROWN RANGE

WA

GREAT VICTORIA DESERT

NEALE BREAKAWAYS

NULLARBOR PLAIN

BAXTER CLIFFS

125°E

METRES
1000
500

SOUTH

NULLARBOR—VICTORIA RIVER DISTRICT

130°E

NORTH

METRES
1000
500

ANSON BAY

VICTORIA RIVER
VICTORIA RIVER DISTRICT

WARE RANGE

TANAMI DESERT

NT

GREAT SANDY DESERT

WESTERN DESERT

BLOODS RANGE
PETERMANN RANGES
MANN RANGES

GREAT VICTORIA DESERT

SA

NULLARBOR PLAIN

BAXTER CLIFFS

130°E

METRES
1000
500

SOUTH

EYRE PENINSULA–ARNHEM LAND

135°E

METRES
1000
500
NORTH

TABOOMA ISLAND
ROPER RIVER
ARNHEM LAND
BARKLY TABLELAND
NT
DAVENPORT RANGE
SANDOVER RIVER
HARTS RANGE
FERGUSSON RANGE
SIMPSON DESERT
CENTRAL AUSTRALIA
TODD RIVER
FINKE RIVER
ALBERGA RIVER
FAR NORTH
STUART RANGE
SA
GAWLER RANGES
EYRE PENINSULA

135°E
METRES
1000
500
SOUTH

LOWER SOUTH-EAST–GULF COUNTRY

140°E

METRES
1000
500
NORTH

LEICHHARDT RIVER
LEICHHARDT RIVER
GULF COUNTRY
SELWYN RANGE
NORTH-WEST QLD
HAMILTON RIVER
CHANNEL COUNTRY
Qld
DIAMANTINA RIVER
STURTS STONY DESERT
COOPERS CREEK
STRZELECKI DESERT
LAKE CALLABONNA
LAKE FROME
SA
BENDA RANGE
MURRAY RIVER
LOWER MURRAY
SOUTH-EAST MALLEE

140°E
METRES
1000
500
SOUTH

WESTERN TASMANIA–CAPE YORK PENINSULA

SOUTH COAST–CENTRAL QUEENSLAND

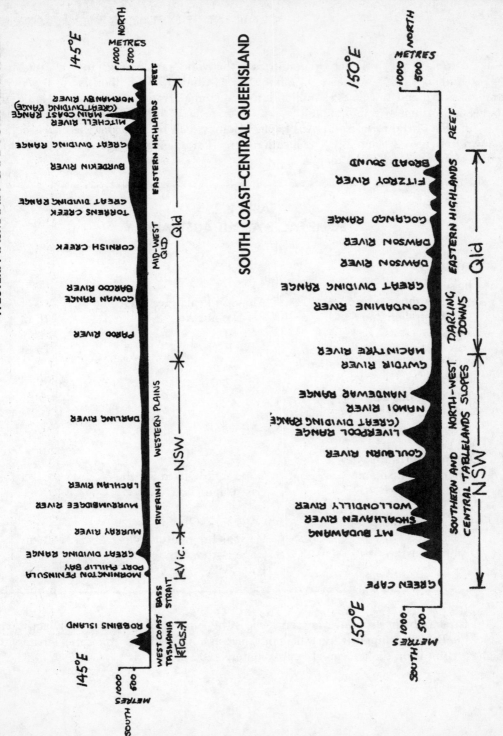

Australia is one of the largest countries in the world, ranking sixth in size after Russia (17.1 million km^2), Canada (9.97 million km^2), China (9.59 million km^2), USA (9.36 million km^2), and Brazil (8.51 million km^2). Australia's Antarctic Territory is large, too, being approximately 8 million km^2.

An idea of the form of the Australian landmass can be see from the cross-sections shown in figures 2.1 and 2.2. The location of the latitudes and longitudes of each of the cross-sections is shown on map 9.

TABLE 2.2
SOME FACTS ABOUT AUSTRALIA

ALTITUDES

Highest point		
—on Australian territory	Mawson Peak, Heard Island	2744 m
—on Australian mainland	Mt Kosciuszko, NSW	2228 m
Lowest point		
—on Australian mainland	Lake Eyre, SA	-15 m
Average altitude of Australian landmass		300 m
Land over 500 m (percentage)		13.0%
Land over 1000 m (percentage)		0.5%

DISTANCES

Distance north to south		
—including Tasmania	Cape York, Qld to South East Cape, Tas.	
3680 km		
—mainland only	Cape York, Qld to Wilsons Promontory, Vic.	3180 km
Distance east to west	Cape Byron, NSW to Steep Point, WA	4000 km

Australia's highest point, Mawson Peak is the summit of Australia's only active volcano, Big Ben, and supports Australia's only glaciers. In Australia's Antarctic Territory the highest point is on the ice cap at approximately 4200 m.

TABLE 2.3
AUSTRALIA'S EXTREME GEOGRAPHICAL COORDINATES

MAINLAND AUSTRALIA
AND TASMANIA

Most northerly point	Cape York, Qld	10° 41'S
Most southerly point	South East Cape, Tas.	43° 39'S
—on Australian mainland	Wilsons Promontory, Vic.	39° 08'S
Most easterly point	Cape Byron, NSW	153° 39'E
Most westerly point	Steep Point, WA	113° 09'E

OFF-SHORE AUSTRALIA

Most northerly point	Bramble Cay, Qld	9° 09'S
Most southerly point	Bishop and Clerk Island, Tas.	55° 06'S
Most easterly point	Norfolk Island	167° 57'E
Most westerly point	Cocos Islands	96° 53'E

AUSTRALIAN ANTARCTIC
TERRITORY

Most northerly point	Enderby Land	66°S approx.
Most southerly point	South Pole	90° 00'S
Most easterly point	eastern 'border' of Victoria Land	160° 00'E
Most westerly point	western 'border' of Princess Elizabeth Land	45° 00'E

The closest island to the southernmost point of Tasmania, and visible from there, is Pedra Blanca, which lies some 25 km south of South East Cape at approximately 43° 51'S. On the west of Australia just a short distance north-north-west of Steep Point, Western Australia, lies the island of Dirk Hartog. The westernmost point of this island lies just south of West Point, at approximately 112° 55'E.

TABLE 2.4
AUSTRALIA'S EXTREME SITINGS OF SETTLEMENT

MOST NORTHERLY

—settlement	Koedal Boepur, Boigu Island, Qld	9° 05'S
—town-1	Christmas Island	10° 25'S
—town-2	Thursday Island, Qld	10° 34'S
—mainland settlement	Seisa, Qld	10° 51'S
—mainland town	Nhulunbuy, NT	12° 18'S

MOST SOUTHERLY

—town	Dover, Tas.	43°19'S
—settlement	Catamaran, Tas.	43° 33'S
—mainland town	Apollo Bay, Vic.	38° 46'S
—mainland settlement	Tidal River, Vic.	39° 02'S

MOST EASTERLY

—settlement	Kingston, Norfolk Island	166° 30'E
—mainland settlement	Byron Bay, NSW	153° 38'E

MOST WESTERLY

—settlement	Home Island, Cocos Islands	96° 04'E
—mainland settlement	Useless Loop, WA	113° 22'E
—mainland town	Denham, WA	113° 32'E

It is possible that the fishing shack settlement at Quobba Point, Western Australia, lies marginally further west than Useless Loop.

Davis, at 68° 35'S, is Australia's southernmost settlement in Australian Antarctic Territory. Other Australian Antarctic Territory stations—Mawson at 62° 52'E and Davis at 77° 58'E—lie further west than the most westerly points listed in table 2.4.

TABLE 2.5
EXTREME GEOGRAPHICAL COORDINATES OF EACH STATE/TERRITORY

NEW SOUTH WALES

North	inland from Point Danger	28° 10'S
South	Cape Howe	37° 31'S
East	Cape Byron	153° 39'E
West	western border	141° 00'E
Off-shore	Wolfe Rock, Lord Howe Island Group	159° 08'E

VICTORIA

North	north-west of Lindsay Point	33° 59'S
South	Wilsons Promontory	39° 08'S
East	Cape Howe	149° 59'E
West	western border	140° 58'E
Off-shore	islands of the Anser Group	39° 12'S

QUEENSLAND

North	Cape York	10° 41'S
South	Beardy-Dumaresq River junction	29° 11'S
East	Point Danger	153° 33'E
West	western border	138° 00'E
Off-shore north	Bramble Cay	9° 09'S
Off-shore east	North Stradbroke Island	153° 33'E

SOUTH AUSTRALIA

North	northern border	26° 00'S
South	Cape Northumberland	38° 04'S
East	eastern border with New South Wales	141° 00'E
West	western border	129° 00'E

WESTERN AUSTRALIA

North	Cape Londonderry	13° 44'S
South	West Cape Howe	35° 08'S
East	eastern border	129° 00'E
West	Steep Point	113° 09'E
Off-shore north	Stewart Island	13° 41'S
Off-shore south	Eclipse Island	35° 11'S
Off-shore west	Dirk Hartog Island	112°55'E

TABLE 2.5
(continued)

TASMANIA

North	Woolnorth Point	40° 38'S
South	South East Cape	43° 39'S
East	Cape Forestier	148° 22'E
West	Bluff Hill Point	144° 36'E
Off-shore north	islands of the Hogan Group	39° 12'S
Off-shore south	Bishop and Clerk Island	55° 06'S
Off-shore east	Macquarie Island	159° 40'E
Off-shore west	King Island	143° 50'E

NORTHERN TERRITORY

North	Smith Point	11° 08'S
South	southern border	26° 00'S
East	eastern border	138° 00'E
West	western border	129° 00'E
Off-shore north	New Year Island	10° 54'S

AUSTRALIAN CAPITAL TERRITORY

North	Hall district	35° 08'S
South	near Mt Clear	35° 55'S
East	place south of Bungendore (NSW)	149° 24'E
West	south of Mt Franklin	148° 46'E

CORAL SEA ISLANDS TERRITORY

North	northern boundary	12° 00'S
South	southern boundary	24° 00'S
East	eastern boundary	157° 10'E
West	near Wreck Bay	144° 00'E approx.

The latitudes and longitudes in table 2.5 for the Australian Capital Territory exclude the Jervis Bay portion of that Territory.

The observant will have noticed that the common borders of Victoria–South Australia and New South Wales–South Australia are not located at the same longitude.

It was intended that both borders would lie along the 141°E meridian. Owing to inaccurate methods used to determine longitude in the 19th century, however, the Victoria–South Australia border failed to meet the New South Wales–South Australia border where they should have met, meeting instead at the Murray River, 3 km west of the meridian. As records show the border to be inaccurate, South Australia has a claim to a slice of Victoria 3 km wide.

Similar problems occurred with the Queensland–Northern Territory border when it was surveyed in the 19th century. Here, the border lies approximately 1 km to the west of the 138°E meridian. The Northern Territory once made a claim for this land but it is generally accepted that boundaries be recognised by practice rather than by latitudes and longitudes.

It is just as well that such amicable dealings exist between State governments; otherwise, New South Wales and Victoria would be in trouble. The boundary between these two States mostly runs along the southern bank of the Murray River but it has sometimes happened that the territory of one State lies on the opposite bank of the river. During times of flood the river sometimes changes course, abandoning some old horseshoe-shaped meander loops and creating new channels. When this occurs, the abandoned loop and adjacent land lie on the opposite bank. Under common law such land is deemed to continue to be part of the State whose land it was originally. For example, Ouranie Island is a little bit of Victoria north of the river, and the locality of Talmalmo is a part of New South Wales situated in Victoria. The next part of Victoria expected to 'cross the border' (it may have already done so) is downstream from Merbein in the Sunraysia district.

TABLE 2.6
EXTREME SITINGS OF SETTLEMENTS FOR STATES/TERRITORIES
AND COORDINATES OF THE CAPITAL CITIES

NEW SOUTH WALES

Capital	Sydney	33° 51'S
		151° 13'E
North	Tweed Heads	28° 11'S
South	Wonboyn	37° 15'S
East	Byron Bay	153° 37'E
West	Burns	141° 00'E
Off-shore	Lord Howe Island	159° 04'E

TABLE 2.6
(continued)

VICTORIA

Capital	Melbourne	37° 49'S
		144° 58'E
North	Yelta	34° 08'S
South	Tidal River	39° 02'S
East	Mallacoota	149° 45'E
West	Serviceton	141° 00'E

QUEENSLAND

Capital	Brisbane	27° 28'S
		153° 02'E
North	Seisa	10° 51'S
South	Wallangarra	28° 56'S
East	Coolangatta	153° 32'E
West	Camooweal	138° 07'E
Off-shore north	Koedal Boepur,	
	Boigu Island	9° 05'S
Off-shore east	Point Lookout,	
	Nth stradbroke Island	153° 33'E

SOUTH AUSTRALIA

Capital	Adelaide	34° 56'S
		138° 35'E
North	Kalka	26° 10'S
South	Port Macdonnell	38° 03'S
East	Cockburn	141° 00'E
West	Travellers Village	129° 00'E

WESTERN AUSTRALIA

Capital	Perth	31° 57'S
		115° 51'E
North	Kalumburu	14° 18'S
South	Albany	35° 02'S
East	Wingelinna	128° 58'E
West	Useless Loop	113° 22'E

TABLE 2.6
(continued)

TASMANIA

Capital	Hobart	42° 53'S
		147° 20'E
North	Stanley	40° 46'S
South	Catamaran	43° 33'S
East	Bicheno	148° 18'E
West	Marrawah	144° 42'E
Off-shore north	Egg Lagoon, King Island	39° 40'S
Off-shore west	Currie, King Island	143° 52'E

NORTHERN TERRITORY

Capital	Darwin	12° 28'S
		130° 51'E
North	Black Point:	
	Cobourg Peninsula	11° 09'S
South	Kulgera	25° 51'S
East	Alpurrurulam	137° 50'E
West	Docker River	129° 06'E
Off-shore	Minjilang, Croker Island	11° 09'S

AUSTRALIAN CAPITAL TERRITORY

Capital	Canberra	35° 17'S
		149° 08'E
North	Jervis Bay Village	35° 08'S
South	Williamsdale	35° 34'S
East	Jervis Bay Village	150° 43'E
West	Uriarra Forestry Camp	148° 58'E

OFF-SHORE AUSTRALIA

North	Christmas Island	10° 25'S
South	Davis, Australian	
	Antarctic Territory	68° 35'S
East	Kingston, Norfolk Island	166° 30'E
West	Home Island, Cocos Islands	96° 54'E

Note that the figures in table 2.6 refer to the coordinates of settlements, not neces-sarily towns. The coordinates for the capital cities are based on the location of their major weather stations.

Australia's plains

Australia is characterised by its plains. A plain is an extensive area of level to slightly undulating country with perhaps only the odd residual hill or rocky outcrop breaking its uniform skyline. There are a number of different types of plains.

Clay plains are quite common in Australia. These slightly undulating plains (some-times called downs) are formed on special types of black, clayey soils that exhibit wide and deep cracks when dry or produce thick gooey ooze when wet. Most of the downs of mid-western Queensland and the Barkly Tableland are clay plains.

Coastal plains are gently sloping plains developed as a result of the shoreline extend-ing at the expense of the sea. Coastal plains are of low relief with perhaps only a few rem-nants of low, residual hills breaking the skyline. The Pilbara coast of Western Australia has good examples of coastal plains.

Lacustrine plains (or lake beds) are large and not so large flat beds of what is nor-mally a dry lake. A variety of surfaces are found on lake beds—salt, clay or gypsum, sometimes with a thin covering of vegetation. On the prevailing downwind side of the lake there may be sand, clay or gypsum dunes (these dunes being called 'lunettes' in southern Australia). Lake Mungo and the Walls of China in western New South Wales is one example of a lacustrine plain and lunette.

Floodplains are plains bordering a river and are formed by deposits of sediment car-ried by that river. During a flood the river rises above its banks, covering the plain with water and sediments. Floodplains support a number of landforms such as stream mean-ders, billabongs and levee banks. Deltas are a special type of floodplain formed where a river enters a lake or the sea—for example, the Burdekin River delta in north Queensland. Small floodplains in hilly country are sometimes known as river flats. There are numerous examples of floodplains throughout Australia, with perhaps the biggest floodplains being found along many of the inland rivers—the Barwon and Gwydir rivers of northern New South Wales, for example, or Cooper Creek below Windorah in Queensland's Channel Country.

A pediplain is a type of plain found on the edges of uplifted mountain ranges. A pediplain slopes away from the range towards the lowlands and there is often a distinct angle of slope between the pediplain and the range. Streams issuing from the mountains may cut into the pediplain or deposit sediment (alluvium) over the plain in the shape of a fan. These are alluvials fans, and they are a type of floodplain. Good examples of pediplains can be seen along the western side of the Flinders Ranges in South Australia.

Peneplains are formed by rivers and rain gradually wearing down or eroding the landscape to such an extent that only the very resistant rocky outcrops or low hills stand above the plain. Peneplains tend to gradually slope towards stream channels, along which there will be a floodplain. Most of the Lake Eyre basin is a vast peneplain.

Riverine or alluvial plains are plains of alluvium (eroded sediments) deposited by rivers either currently (hence they are floodplains) or some time in the past. Riverine plains tend to be relatively featureless—just immense expanses of dead-level uniformity interrupted at intervals by shallow, but normally dry watercourses. Much of the Riverina region of New South Wales and the adjacent districts of north-central Victoria are riverine plains.

Sandplains are Australia's most widespread type of plain. Dominated by vast sheets of sand, they exhibit either broad and low sandy rises barely a metre high, such as is found in the Tanami Desert of the Northern Territory, or sand dunes up to 20 m high. The dunes are mostly longitudinal, with margins stabilised by vegetation but with mobile and oscillating crests subjected to movement by winds. Longitudinal dunes may be hundreds of kilometres long. Between each dune there are flat areas, or swales, up to a kilometre wide and covered with sand or occasionally stones. Most of Australia's named deserts are dune-covered sandplains—for instance, the Simpson Desert or Great Sandy Desert.

Shield plains exhibit both rocky and sandy surfaces. Normally there are two levels of plain separated by a low, rocky cliff less than 15 m high, which is called a breakaway. Normally the upper plain is slightly undulating with outcrops of stone, usually granite, with occasional low, rocky rises, while the lower plain is generally flat and sandy. Shield plains are enormous and widespread in the south-western quarter of Western Australia and are also found in Central Australia.

Stony plains come in two types: gibbers or sheets of rock. Gibber plains are slightly undulating, and covered with countless billions of small to not so small pebbles. They are found near old, low tablelands (known as 'jump-ups') or as rolling stony downs. In arid areas gibber plains form Australia's most desolate landscapes—for instance, Sturts Stony Desert and parts of the Channel Country of Queensland. Rock plains occur as expansive sheets of rock, the best-known example being the Nullarbor Plain. This ever-so-slightly undulating plain of limestone has minor features such as sinkholes and caves.

Tidal plains are coastal plains subjected to inundation by the sea. They are flat with perhaps some residual relict dunes rising above the general level of the plain, and are coursed by wildly meandering estuaries, normally outlets of major river systems. Tidal plains are common along the southern shoreline of the Gulf of Carpentaria.

Volcanic plains are formed by vast outpourings of lava, which cover the pre-existing landscape. They are generally undulating and support volcanic features such as old craters, stony rises (solidified lava flows), lava tubes and volcanic lakes. Most of the Western Districts of Victoria is a volcanic plain, as is the McBride Volcanic Province of the North-East Highlands of Queensland.

TABLE 2.7
SOME AUSTRALIAN PLAINS: BY SIZE

Lake Eyre peneplain, Qld–SA–NT	1,170,000 km²
Nullarbor Plain, SA–WA	270,000 km²
Barkly Tableland, Qld–NT	240,000 km²
North-West Plains, NSW–Qld	145,000 km²
Hay Plains, NSW	70,000 km²
lava plains west of Melbourne, Vic.	23,000 km²
Mundi Mundi Plain, NSW–SA	4,300 km²
Willochra Plain, SA	3,000 km²
Adelaide Plains, SA	1,500 km²

The areas given in table 2.7 for the plains are approximate, owing to problems in defining boundaries.

The distances in table 2.8 refer to dead-straight roads, those without even the slightest bends. Such roads are found in plains country. There are many roads crossing Australian plains that are nearly dead straight but most have slight bends at 15–25 km intervals in order to help keep the driver alert. For instance, the Mitchell Highway between Nyngan and Bourke, New South Wales, is always shown dead straight on the road maps, but has slight bends at regular intervals. The original figure I found for the Victorian section of the Sturt Highway west of Culluleraine was 75 km but realignments have shortened this distance.

THE LAKE EYRE BASIN IS A VAST PENEPLAIN. IT IS THE LARGEST INLAND CATCHMENT AREA IN AUSTRALIA (SEE TABLE 5.2). THE PLAIN ITSELF, CONSTITUTING THIS BASIN, IS CONSIDERED TO BE THE LARGEST PENE-PLAIN IN THE WORLD.

Determining Queensland's straightest road is tricky: the Landsborough Highway between Barcaldine and Ilfracombe goes close but has slight bends. The figure for South Australia is unreliable. The minor road between Comet and Indooroopilly outstations, north of Tarcoola, may be longer while the old unsealed route of the Eyre Highway near Koonalda Station on the Nullarbor Plain was about 86 km long.

Western Australia is the place for dead-straight roads; the North-West Coastal Highway between the Murchison River and Carnarvon has a few very long straights. The Eyre Highway figure given in table 2.8 is probably a world record; as a matter of interest, a track following an old telegraph line east of Caiguna extended this figure by another 68 km, giving a total length of 216 km.

TABLE 2.8
STRAIGHTEST ROAD IN EACH STATE/TERRITORY

NSW	Mitchell Highway, Nevertire–Nyngan	59	km
Vic.	Sturt Highway, west of Cululleraine	25	km
Qld	information unavailable		
SA	Oodnadatta Track, Warriners–Engenina Creeks	71	km
WA	Eyre Highway, Caiguna–east of Balladonia	148	km
Tas.	Evandale Road, Nile–Evandale	9.5	km
NT	Barkly Highway, Frewena–Dalmore Downs Stn	63	km
ACT	Northbourne Avenue, Canberra	4.1 km	

TABLE 2.9
STRAIGHTEST SECTION OF RAILWAY IN EACH STATE/TERRITORY

NSW	Nevertire–Nyngan, Main West Line	64.5 km
Vic.	Violet Town–Benalla, Albury Line	21.7 km
Qld	Barcaldine–Longreach, Central Line	76.5 km
SA	Ooldea–WA border, Trans-Continental Line	254.0 km
WA	SA border–Nurina, Trans-Continental Line	223.0 km
Tas.	west of Launceston, Western Line	6.6 km
NT	north of Kulgera, Central Australian Line	21.9 km
ACT	Queanbeyan–Canberra, Canberra Line	1.0 km

Before falling into disuse, the Main West Line between Nyngan and Bourke, New South Wales, was the third-longest straight stretch of railway in the world, at 186 km. In New South Wales there are other long, straight stretches: on the Broken Hill Line there are three straights each over 70 km long, while between Narromine and Bourke, Main West Line, there were only five curves in 327 km.

The figure given in table 2.9 for the Australian Capital Territory's straightest section of railway is exceeded by a stretch 4.3 km long on the old Cooma Line between Royalla and Williamsdale, where the line forms part of the common border with New South Wales.

Australian deserts

Another distinguishing feature of Australia is its deserts. Defining a desert is difficult, however: if based on rainfall (average falls totalling less than 250 mm per year is the normal measurement), then about half of Australia is desert. If, on the other hand, the definition is based on a virtual absence of vegetation, then hardly any of Australia is desert.

Australian deserts are better described as arid lands. What characterises them is low and erratic rainfall, a relatively sparse covering of vegetation in many but not all areas, and countryside deemed unsuitable for the grazing of stock because of unpalatable spinifex grasses or extensive dune systems. Most named Australian deserts are sand-dune-covered plains—those distinguished by longitudinal dunes with flat areas (swales) between—for instance, the Great Victoria Desert. Some other named deserts are stony deserts: for example, the Gibson Desert.

TABLE 2.10
AUSTRALIA'S DESERTS: BY SIZE

Great Sandy Desert, WA–NT	longitudinal dunes	414,000 km^2
Great Victoria Desert, SA–WA	longitudinal dunes	325,000 km^2
Tanami Desert, WA–NT	sandplain	310,000 km^2
Simpson Desert, Qld–SA–NT	longitudinal dunes	170,000 km^2
Little Sandy Desert, WA	longitudinal dunes	30,000 km^2
Sturts Stony Desert, Qld–SA	stony	20,000 km^2
Gibson Desert, WA	stony	20,000 km^2
Strzelecki Desert, NSW–SA	longitudinal dunes	5,000 km^2
Tirari Desert, SA	sand dunes	5,000 km^2

Owing to problems in defining boundaries, the area of each desert included in table 2.10 is approximate, being only indicative of its size. For instance, one source gives the area of the Great Victoria Desert as 420,000 km^2. Furthermore, I believe the Strzelecki Desert to be larger than the figure quoted above, and that Sturts Stony Desert is indistinguishable from the stony plains that comprise much of the arid regions of Queensland's Channel Country. Not included above is the unnamed sand-dune desert in the Northern Territory south of the Barkly Tableland.

Australia has other named deserts, which have no specific geographic location, such as the Western Desert and the Central Desert. The Western Desert is sometimes used to mean the Great Sandy, Gibson and Great Victoria Deserts combined, or the sandy desert country south-west and west of Alice Springs, Northern Territory, centred around Lake Amadeus, Uluru and the Petermann-Rawlinson Ranges. The Central Desert refers to the arid country north of Alice Springs and may include parts of the Tanami Desert and the sandplains along the Sandover River.

Other named deserts which have occasionally been described include the Meekatharra Desert, covering the stony arid lands to the north-west of Meekatharra, Western Australia; the Canning Desert, which is another name for the Great Sandy Desert; the Arunta Desert, best known as the Simpson Desert.

There are other tracts of land with the name 'desert', too. There is the Little Desert (1300 km^2), in Victoria; nearby, also in Victoria, there is the Big Desert, which adjoins the Ninety-Mile Desert in South Australia (combined area: 7000 km^2)—all these areas being uncleared mallee eucalypt country with sand dunes. In Western Australia the Pinnacles Desert, lying north of Perth, is an area of coastal dunes exhibiting an array of limestone pinnacles. Elsewhere, there are other 'deserts': the so-called 'desert uplands'— spinifex and stunted eucalypts lying just to the east of the road between Aramac and Torrens Creek in mid-west Queensland. There is also the so-called 'wet desert', an area of open heaths on Cape York Peninsula. Nearby, north-west of Laura, Cape York Peninsula, is an area simply called 'The Desert'. All of these areas are not strictly deserts, in terms of aridity, but were so-named by early pastoralists as tracts of country unsuitable for the grazing of stock.

In South Australia, north-east of the Flinders Ranges near Lake Blanche, is The Cobbler, a small desert of clay knoblets and shifting dunes formed by the voracious appetite of rabbits devouring the vegetation.

THE LONGEST STRAIGHT STRETCH OF RAILWAY IN THE WORLD IS THE TRANS-CONTINENTAL LINE MENTIONED IN TABLE 2.9: ITS COMBINED TOTAL LENGTH IS 477 KM.

TABLE 2.11
AUSTRALIA'S DESERT TRACKS

Canning Stock Route	Wiluna–Halls Creek, WA	1820 km
Kidson or Wapet Track-Papunya Track	Sandfire Flat Roadhouse–Papunya, WA–NT	1645 km
Anne Beadell Highway	Coober Pedy–Laverton, SA–WA	1342 km
Talawana/Windy Corner Tracks-Gary, Gunbarrel, Heather Highways	Newman–Warburton, WA	1039 km
Colson Track-French Line-QAA Line	Alice Springs–Birdsville, NT–SA–Qld	778 km
Rig Road-Birdsville Track	Mt Dare–Birdsville, SA–Qld	773 km
Anne Beadell Highway-Mt Lindsay Track	Coober Pedy–Pipalyatjara, SA	730 km
Rig Road-K1 Line-QAA Line	Mt Dare–Birdsville, SA–Qld	701 km
Connie Sue Highway	Warburton–Rawlinna, WA	581 km
French Line-QAA Line	Mt Dare–Birdsville, SA–Qld	507 km
Gunbarrel-Heather Highways	Carnegie Station–Warburton, WA	492 km

Do not be fooled by the name 'highway' for some of these routes: these are all unmaintained desert tracks. Australia's deserts are remote places and intending travellers on these routes should note that crossings are not to be lightly undertaken. In some instances convoy travel with an experienced leader is required, as well as permits. All routes are strictly 4WD.

The original Gunbarrel Highway, travel over parts of which is restricted today, ran between Victory Downs Station, Northern Territory, and Carnegie Station, Western Australia—a distance of approximately 1400 km. The Kidson or Wapet Track-Papunya Track gives access to two of Australia's remotest Aboriginal settlements: Kiwirrkurra and Kunawarratji.

Just to confuse the issue, table 2.12 lists Australia's famous desert and other outback tracks, most of which have been upgraded into two-lane, gravel and earth outback main roads. All these roads are suitable for travel in conventional vehicles during dry conditions with care and some outback driving experience. Distances are measured between settlements at the end of, or beyond the named route and the table also shows the average number of vehicles per day using these routes.

TABLE 2.12
SOME FAMOUS OUTBACK ROADS

ROAD	ROUTE	DISTANCE	VEHICLES /DAY
Tanami Road	Alice Springs–Halls Creek, NT–WA	1,012 km	(20)
Gulf Track	Burketown–Roper Bar, Qld–NT	873 km	(10)
Plenty-Donahue Highways	Alice Springs–Boulia, NT–Qld	821 km	(25)
Sandover Highway	Alice Springs–Camooweal, NT–Qld	813 km	(5)
Buchanan Highway	Dunmurra–Halls Creek, NT–WA	767 km	(10)
Gibb River Road	Derby–Wyndham, WA	715 km	(45)
Oodnadatta Track	Marree–Marla, SA	614 km	(25)
Duncan Highway	Halls Creek–Timber Creek, WA–NT	610 km	(5)
Birdsville Track	Marree–Birdsville, SA–Qld	593 km	(20)
Warburton Road	Laverton–Warburton, WA–NT	565 km	(10)
Strzelecki Track	Lyndhurst–Innamincka, SA	467 km	(45)

The Warburton Road (Table 2.12) has recently been called the Great Central Road, this name extending it to include the route between Warburton and Yulara, Northern Teritory—a total distance of 1141 km.

THREE

THE LAND: HILLS, MOUNTAINS AND TABLELANDS

The land is a complex of phenomena—a rich tapestry of rocks, soils and plant life, which assumes different forms at different places for different reasons. The major observable fact about the land is the way it lies. It forms a continuous surface, virtually level in some places and moderately or steeply sloping at others. This surface is dissected by stream channels and its edges are delineated by coastlines. As an integral part of this surface, there are numerous landforms, the origin of which has involved a number of interacting elements.

Creation of landscapes

Physical landscapes are controlled by their underlying structure or geology. The geology of a landscape varies from place to place. In some places it is partially or completely exposed, especially in arid areas or where there is minimal vegetation cover; at other places it is buried by deposits of previously transported and eroded rock materials. This erosion, transportation and deposition of materials is what creates landscapes. The main agents of erosion in Australia are water and wind. Ice in the form of glaciers has also played a part in sculpturing Australian landscapes, but only a small one (mainly in Tasmania). Since European occupation land clearances have accelerated the erosive processes because, after clearing, the land itself is left exposed to the agents of erosion.

Rock materials themselves are broken down through a series of complex processes known, collectively, as 'weathering'. Weathering is the process in which the atmosphere interacts with rock materials. One result of weathering is rock disintegration: larger rock particles are broken into smaller rock particles, which are then capable of being transported by water or wind (and ice, too). Weathering may also result in rock alteration, whereby rock materials—in conjunction with other elements such as climatic or vegetative influences—produce soils.

The net result of weathering and erosion of the land by natural processes that have been occurring virtually uninterrupted for extended periods of time is that the surface of the land becomes lower in altitude. The physical landscape of today is at the same time an original surface (for the processes of natural erosion and deposition are still occurring) and a relict or historical surface which is the result of previous interacting natural processes.

MOUNTAINS AND TABLELANDS

Mountain building

The land can rise, although these processes are usually very slow. The earth's crust—the uppermost level, upon which we live—extends downwards about 8–10 km and is in a state of flux. It moves, and as it makes major or minor adjustments a number of geological or structural forms arise. These structures—which include, for instance, folding and faulting—ultimately become the dominating controls of the physical landscape. Folding is where rock layers are thrust up in wave-like forms. Faulting is where layers of rock are fractured.

Excellent examples of folding can be seen east of Alice Springs in the MacDonnell Ranges, along Bitter Springs Creek. A good example of a fault lies to the immediate west of Lake George, along the Sydney–Canberra highway. Many of Australia's mountain ranges are the result of such folding and faulting—for instance, the Flinders Ranges, South Australia; the Stirling Range, Western Australia; the MacDonnell Ranges, Northern Territory. Different types of mountains occur elsewhere.

Tablelands

Most of Australia's mountain uplands are tablelands (or plateaus—both words mean the same) and are characterised by virtually level to moderately undulating skylines, often bounded by steep, sometimes vertical escarpments. The escarpment edges may be coursed by streams which create either waterfalls or, if incised into the tableland, gorges and canyons. Good examples of these features can be seen in the Blue Mountains, New South Wales. Some tableland surfaces are capped with basalt or lava flows, which form relatively higher summits—the Atherton Tableland in Queensland being a good example. Other well-known tablelands include the Hamersley Range, Western Australia, and the Arnhem Land Plateau, Northern Territory. Interestingly, early explorers and pioneers used the name 'range' for these tablelands, as from a distance their escarpments do appear to be ranges.

Other types of tablelands may be formed by large granite intrusions. These originate deep within the earth's crust and are slowly uplifted above the original surface, where

AUSTRALIA'S LARGEST EXPOSED, SINGULAR GRANITE OUTCROP IS BALD ROCK, NORTHERN TABLELANDS, NEW SOUTH WALES, STANDING 200 M HIGH.

they then are eroded. This erosion process leaves behind high, granite massifs (granite outcrops), such as the Mt Buffalo Plateau in Victoria or much of the Northern Tablelands in New South Wales. Granite formations are often characterised by granite boulders (or tors), balancing rocks or massive granite domes—for instance, the southern coastline of Western Australia between Albany and east of Esperance.

Heights in feet have been given for the mountains in the following tables (3.1–3.6). Altitudes in feet are still used by the aviation industry and many people, myself included, feel that a measurement in metres for mountains lacks a certain aesthetic quality. The imperial measurement of the foot has historical roots relating to the physical world, unlike the metric measurement, which is purely scientific. Besides, mountains measured in feet seem to be bigger!

FIGURE 3.1
COMPARATIVE SIZES OF THE HIGHEST MOUNTAINS IN EACH STATE/TERRITORY

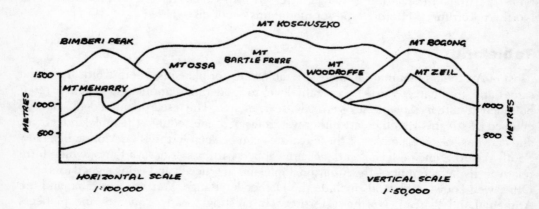

Based on topographic maps, except Mts Meharry, Woodroffe and Zeil

TABLE 3.1
HIGHEST MOUNTAIN IN EACH STATE/TERRITORY

NSW	Mt Kosciuszko, Snowy Mountains	7309 ft	2228 m
Vic.	Mt Bogong, Victorian Alps	6515 ft	1986 m
Qld	Mt Bartle Frere, Bellenden Ker Range	5285 ft	1611 m
SA	Mt Woodroffe, Musgrave Ranges	4721 ft	1439 m
WA	Mt Meharry, Hamersley Range	4104 ft	1251 m
Tas.	Mt Ossa, Cradle Mountain-Lake St Clair National Park	5305 ft	1617 m
NT	Mt Zeil, MacDonnell Ranges	5022 ft	1531 m
ACT	Bimberi Peak, Bimberi Range	6276 ft	1913 m
OSA	Mawson Peak (Big Ben), Heard Island	9002 ft	2744 m

Cross-sections of each of the highest mountains can be seen in figure 3.1.

The highest mountain of the Australian Capital Territory, Bimberi Peak, shares a common border with New South Wales. The highest point of the Australian Antarctic Territory lies on the Antarctic plateau at approximately 4200 m.

TABLE 3.2
THE '7000 FOOTERS'
PEAKS AND TOPS ABOVE 7000 FT IN NEW SOUTH WALES

Mt Kosciuszko	7309 ft	2228 m
Mt Townsend	7249 ft	2209 m
Mt Twynam	7207 ft	2196 m
Mt Alice-Rawson	7200 ft	2194 m
Rams Head	7193 ft	2192 m
Mt Etheridge	7188 ft	2190 m
North Rams Head	7142 ft	2177 m
Mt Lee	7100 ft	2164 m
Abbott Peak	7100 ft	2164 m
unnamed peak near North Rams Head	7050 ft	2148 m
Carruthers Peak	7042 ft	2146 m

All the mountains and hill summits listed in table 3.2 lie within the Snowy Mountains region on the Kosciuszko Plateau. Many tops rise only a few hundred metres above the general level of the plateau upon which they stand. The western fall of this plateau forms the highest hillslope in Australia. Even though Australia's mountains are not really high, the effect of the relatively rarefied air at these altitudes can certainly be felt by anyone undertaking physical activity there: a shortness of breath is common until one adjusts.

TABLE 3.3
THE '6000 FOOTERS'
PEAKS AND TOPS ABOVE 6000 FT IN VICTORIA

Mt Bogong	6515 ft	1986 m
Mt Feathertop	6306 ft	1922 m
Mt Nelse North Peak	6178 ft	1883 m
Mt Fainter South Peak	6158 ft	1877 m
Mt Loch	6148 ft	1874 m
Mt Hotham	6101 ft	1860 m
Mt Niggerhead	6046 ft	1843 m
Mt McKay	6043 ft	1842 m
Mt Cope	6027 ft	1837 m
Mt Fainter North Peak	6027 ft	1837 m
Spion Kopje	6025 ft	1836 m
Mt Cobberas	6025 ft	1836 m

The summits in table 3.3 are all found within the Victorian Alps, mostly in the vicinity of the Bogong High Plains, which is really a plateau. They barely rise 100 m above these plains. Mt Feathertop, on the other hand, is a striking mountain, especially when snow-covered in winter. When viewed from the west near Bright, this is considered to be the most 'alpine-looking' mountain on the Australian mainland. Mt Bogong is also impressive, when seen from the Kiewa Valley. Pedants should note that Bogong West Peak (6447 ft or 1965 m) has been included with Mt Bogong.

In table 3.4 only major peaks, rather than multiple summits, have been listed.

TABLE 3.4
HIGHEST MOUNTAINS: OTHER STATES/TERRITORIES

QUEENSLAND

1 Mt Bartle Frere, Bellenden Ker Range	5285 ft	1611 m
2 Bellenden Ker South Peak, Bellenden Ker Range	5220 ft	1591 m
3 Mt Carbine, Main Coast Range	4650 ft	1417 m

SOUTH AUSTRALIA

1 Mt Woodroffe, Musgrave Ranges	4721 ft	1439 m
2 Mt Charles, Mann Ranges	4370 ft	1332 m
3 Mt Morris, Musgrave Ranges	4113 ft	1254 m

WESTERN AUSTRALIA

1 Mt Meharry, Hamersley Range	4104 ft	1251 m
2 Mt Bruce, Hamersley Range	4026 ft	1227 m
3 Mt Frederick, Hamersley Range	4026 ft	1227 m

TASMANIA

1 Mt Ossa, Cradle Mountain-Lake St Clair National Park	5305 ft	1617 m
2 Legges Tor, Ben Lomond Plateau	5160 ft	1573 m
3 Mt Pelion West, Cradle Mountain-Lake St Clair National Park	5150 ft	1570 m

NORTHERN TERRITORY

1 Mt Zeil, MacDonnell Ranges	5022 ft	1531 m
2 Mt Liebig, Amunurunga Range	5000 ft	1524 m
3 Mt Edward, Belt Range	4646 ft	1416 m

AUSTRALIAN CAPITAL TERRITORY

1 Bimberi Peak, Bimberi Range	6276 ft	1913 m
2 Mt Gingera, Brindabella Range	6092 ft	1838 m
3 Mt Murray, Bimberi Range	6053 ft	1845 m

TABLE 3.5
HIGHEST MOUNTAINS: AUSTRALIAN ISLANDS

Mawson Peak (Big Ben), Heard Island	9002 ft	2744 m
Mt Bowen, Hinchinbrook Island, Qld	3750 ft	1143 m
Mt Gower, Lord Howe Island, NSW	2838 ft	865 m
Strzelecki Peak, Flinders Island, Tas.	2549 ft	777 m
Mt Lidgbird, Lord Howe Island, NSW	2503 ft	763 m
Mt Munro, Cape Barren Island, Tas.	2349 ft	716 m
Mt Maria, Maria Island, Tas.	2326 ft	709 m
Mt Bruny, Bruny Island, Tas.	1883 ft	574 m
Balls Pyramid, Lord Howe Island Group, NSW	1840 ft	561 m
Mt Hamilton, Macquarie Island, Tas.	1420 ft	433 m

So far as table 3.5 is concerned, many of Australia's islands are rugged and mountainous. Those near the mainland coastline can be considered to be formerly part of the mainland during times of lower sea levels, the intervening valleys being flooded by rising seas after the last ice age.

TABLE 3.6
HEIGHTS OF SOME WELL-KNOWN PEAKS

NEW SOUTH WALES

Point Lookout, Northern Tablelands	5249 ft	1600 m
Mt Barrington, Barrington Tops	5101 ft	1555 m
Mt Kaputar, Nandewar Range	5000 ft	1524 m
Mt Canobolas, Central Tablelands	4580 ft	1396 m
Mt Warning, North Coast	3750 ft	1143 m
Mt King-George, Blue Mountains	3471 ft	1058 m
Mt Imlay, South Coast	2904 ft	885 m
Mt Gibraltar, Southern Tablelands	2831 ft	863 m
Pidgeon-House, Budawang Range	2362 ft	720 m
Cambewarra Mountain, Cambewarra Range	2050 ft	625 m

TABLE 3.6 (continued)

VICTORIA

The Horn, Mt Buffalo Plateau	5653 ft	1723 m
Mt William, The Grampians	3829 ft	1167 m
Mt Macedon, Great Dividing Range	3317 ft	1011 m
Mt Buangor, Great Dividing Range	3247 ft	990 m
Mt Dandenong, Dandenong Range	2077 ft	633 m

QUEENSLAND

Thornton Peak, Thornton Range	4511 ft	1375 m
Mt Dalrymple, Clarke Range	4190 ft	1277 m
Mt Lindesay, McPherson Range	3914 ft	1193 m
Mt Cordeaux, Great Dividing Range	3724 ft	1135 m
Mt Beerwah, Glasshouse Mountains	1824 ft	556 m

SOUTH AUSTRALIA

St Marys Peak, Flinders Ranges	3822 ft	1165 m
Rawnsley Bluff, Flinders Ranges	3199 ft	975 m
Mt Remarkable, Flinders Ranges	3150 ft	960 m
Mt Lofty, Mt Lofty Ranges	2384 ft	727 m

WESTERN AUSTRALIA

Mt Augustus, Gascoyne	3625 ft	1105 m
Bluff Knoll, Stirling Range	3596 ft	1096 m
Peak Charles, Yilgarn	2160 ft	658 m
Twin Peaks, The Porongurups	2145 ft	654 m

TASMANIA

Cradle Mountain, Cradle Mountain-Lake St Clair National Park	5065 ft	1544 m
Frenchmans Cap, The South-West	4756 ft	1450 m
Mt Anne, The South-West	4675 ft	1425 m
Mt Wellington, near Hobart	4165 ft	1270 m
Mt Roland, Central Plateau	4039 ft	1231 m
Federation Peak, The South-West	4009 ft	1222 m
Precipitous Bluff, The South-West	4000 ft	1219 m
Millers Bluff, Central Plateau	3977 ft	1212 m

TABLE 3.6 (continued)

NORTHERN TERRITORY		
Mt Olga (Kata Tjuta), Central Australia	3507 ft	1069 m
Ayers Rock (Uluru), Central Australia	2845 ft	867 m
Mt Conner (Atila), Central Australia	2833 ft	863 m
Central Mt Stuart, Central Australia	2770 ft	844 m
AUSTRALIAN CAPITAL TERRITORY		
Mt Franklin, Brindabella Range	5400 ft	1646 m
Tidbinbilla Peak, Tidbinbilla Range	5300 ft	1615 m
Mt Ainslie, Southern Tablelands	2763 ft	842 m

Table 3.6 has been compiled on the basis that each of the peaks generally rises well above its surrounding lowlands and hence is a prominent feature in the landscape. Mt Olga (Kata Tjuta), for instance, rises 546 m above the plain; Ayers Rock (Uluru) rises 348 m and Mt Conner, 300 m.

AYERS ROCK IS THE WORLD'S LARGEST ROCK.

A free-standing mountain is one unattached to other mountains or ridges, and Australia's highest is probably Walshs Pyramid, near Gordonvale, Queensland, which rises about 910 m. The locals claim it is the highest in the world but I very much doubt it. Prominent peaks that give the appearance of being free-standing from certain angles include: Mt Kaputar, New South Wales, which rises 1300 m on its western side above the plain; Bluff Knoll in the Stirling Range, Western Australia, rising about 950 m above the plains; the very grand Mt Augustus, Western Australia. Mt Augustus was previously considered to be the world's largest rock but it is not really one rock, like Ayers Rock (Uluru) is; rather, it is a free-standing and partially vegetated fold in the earth's crust. Nevertheless, it is big, and stands 858 m above the broad Lyons River valley.

AUSTRALIA'S HIGHEST FREE-STANDING MOUNTAIN IS PROBABLY WALSHS PYRAMID NEAR GORDONVALE, QLD — AT ABOUT 910 M ABOVE THE SURROUNDING LOWLANDS.

Wilsons Peak, McPherson Range, New South Wales–Queensland, standing 1231 m high, is unique in Australia inasmuch that rain falling upon its summit can flow into three different States: via the Clarence River into New South Wales; via various creeks to Moreton Bay, Queensland; via Queensland's Condamine River to eventually reach the Murray River in South Australia.

Occupying the high country

THE PEOPLE OF WYCHEPROOF, VICTORIA, LAY CLAIM TO THE WORLD'S LOWEST MOUNTAIN—MT WYCHEPROOF, WHICH IS 149 M HIGH.

Although the Australian high country is only of moderate elevation, it is still significant in such a flat land inasmuch as mountainous uplands and tablelands locally modify climate and weather patterns, providing cooler climates for particular agricultural and grazing pursuits. These uplands support numerous local environments and ecological niches, and are the major water catchment areas.

The European occupation of Australia's high country has impacted on these uplands. Tables 3.7–3.12 (following) show the highest-located structures, buildings, settlements, towns, roads and railways in Australia and in each State/Territory.

TABLE 3.7
HIGHEST-LOCATED STRUCTURE IN EACH STATE/TERRITORY

NSW	Seamans Hut, near Mt Kosciuszko	2035 m
Vic.	Summit Hut, near Mt Bogong	1940 m
Qld	Bellenden Ker Tower, near Cairns	1593 m
SA	probably on Mt Lofty, Mt Lofty Ranges	727m
WA	Mt Nameless Tower, near Tom Price	1126 m
Tas.	huts on Legges Tor, Ben Lomond Plateau	1560 m
NT	tower above Heavitree Gap, near Alice Springs	750 m
ACT	Mt Ginini Tower, Brindabella Range	1762 m

The human-made structure actually located at the greatest altitude in Australia is the cairn on top of Mt Kosciuszko, situated at 2220 m. The Summit Hut near Mt Bogong has been destroyed by fire.

In a building constructed on top of Mt Kosciuszko by the meteorologist Clement Wragge (known as 'Inclement' to his friends), he and other meteorologists recorded the weather and other atmospheric conditions between 1897 and 1901. In winter the temperatures fell to -15° C and winds up to 225 km/hr were recorded.

TABLE 3.8
AUSTRALIA'S HIGHEST SETTLEMENTS

Thredbo-Crackenback, NSW	highest alpine service area	1957 m
Blue Cow, NSW	alpine service area	1880 m
Charlottes Pass, NSW	highest alpine village	1758 m
Mt Hotham, Vic.	highest winter trafficable alpine village	1750 m
Perisher Valley, NSW	alpine village	1730 m
Smiggin Holes, NSW	alpine village	1675 m
Wire Plain, Vic.	alpine service area	1650 m
Guthega, NSW	alpine village	1640 m
Mt Selwyn, NSW	alpine service area	1590 m
Dinner Plain, Vic.	alpine village	1585 m
Falls Creek, Vic.	alpine village	1580 m
Mt Buller, Vic.	alpine village	1560 m
Mt Baw Baw, Vic.	alpine village	1524 m
Diggers Creek, NSW	alpine hotel	1520 m
Tatra Inn, Vic.	alpine hotel	1510 m
Cabramurra, NSW	highest small town	1460 m
Ben Lomond, Tas.	alpine service area	1440 m
Dingo Dell, Vic.	alpine service area	1410 m
Kiandra, NSW	ghost township	1396 m
Wilsons Valley, NSW	alpine hotel	1372 m
Thredbo, NSW	alpine village	1370 m
Ben Lomond, NSW	highest farming township	1363 m
Ebor, NSW	farming township	1348 m
Lake Mountain, Vic.	alpine service area	1340 m
Mt Buffalo, Vic.	alpine hotel	1331 m
Black Mountain, NSW	farming township	1320 m
Guyra, NSW	highest country town	1319 m
Mt St Gwinear, Vic.	alpine service area	1280 m
Shooters Hill, NSW	farming locality	1250 m
Mt Stirling, Vic.	alpine service area	1250 m
Mt Donna Buang, Vic.	alpine service area	1250 m
Black Springs, NSW	farming township	1220 m
Sawpit Creek, NSW	national park settlement	1200 m
Mt Field, Tas.	alpine service area	1200 m

TABLE 3.9
HIGHEST SETTLEMENT IN EACH STATE/TERRITORY

NSW	Thredbo-Crackenback	alpine service area	1957 m
Vic.	Mt Hotham	alpine village	1750 m
Qld	Tumoulin	township	965 m
SA	Mt Lofty	tourist complex	727 m
WA	Tom Price	mining town	740 m
Tas.	Ben Lomond	alpine service area	1440 m
NT	Areyonga	Aboriginal settlement	672 m
ACT	Williamsdale	roadhouse	745 m

The settlements listed in tables 3.8 and 3.9 include all localities as well as townships and small towns.

The store at Evelyn Central in Queensland's north-east highlands, at 1085 m, was this State's highest settlement until it closed down.

By way of comparison, the highest Aboriginal camp site yet discovered lies on a saddle below Perisher Gap, in the Snowy Mountains, New South Wales, at an altitude of 1830 m.

TABLE 3.10
HIGHEST TOWN OR TOWNSHIP IN EACH STATE/TERRITORY

NSW	Cabramurra	small hydro-electricity township	1460 m
Vic.	Bendoc	small farming and timber township	840 m
Qld	Ravenshoe	farming town	910 m
SA	Blinman	old mining township	616 m
WA	Tom Price	mining town	740 m
Tas.	Miena	small township	1037 m
NT	Alice Springs	regional centre	579 m
ACT	Canberra	federal capital city	560 m

The figure in table 3.10 for Canberra is for the centre of the city.

Determining the highest town in Victoria was not easy, owing to the fact that the interesting hill-station town of Mt Macedon ranges in altitude from 550 m to 860 m. Its upper portions are therefore higher than Bendoc, but the 'centre' of Mt Macedon is about 620 m above sea level and so it is beaten by Stanley (760 m), Lyonville (760 m), Benambra (700 m) and Omeo (680 m), as well by Trentham, Tolmie and Bullarto. In East Gippsland the Seldom Seen garage and store near Wulgulmerang is situated 900 m above sea level, but this settlement hardly constitutes a township. Although offering little indication of a township today, the old mining settlement of Grant in the Victorian Alps, was 1140 m above sea level. Another old mining settlement in Victoria, Aberfeldy, was located at a height of 1090 m.

TABLE 3.11
HIGHEST ROADS IN EACH STATE/TERRITORY
(roads open to the public)

NEW SOUTH WALES

Kosciuszko Summit Road at Charlottes Pass	1830 m
Smiggin Holes–Guthega Link Road north of Smiggin Holes	1710 m
Kings Cross Loop Road at Kings Cross, near Cabramurra	1610 m
Khancoban–Kiandra Road near Round Mountain	1600 m
Alpine Way, at Dead Horse Gap	1590 m

VICTORIA

Alpine Road near Mt Hotham	1830 m
Pretty Valley Pondage Road near the Ruined Castle	1780 m
Cope Road near Mt Cope	1720 m
Mt Buller Summit Road at the summit	1676 m
Howitt High Plains Road near Snowy Range landing ground	1630 m
Dargo High Plains Road on the Dargo High Plains	1628 m

QUEENSLAND

Tumoulin Road near Kennedy Highway turnoff	1143 m
Kennedy Highway near Tumoulin turnoff	1130 m
Herberton Road near Kennedy Highway turnoff	986 m
Amiens Road near Pozieres (Stanthorpe district)	961 m
Palmerston Highway at Kennedy Highway junction	960 m
Kennedy Development Road 90 km south of The Lynd	941 m

TABLE 3.11 (continued)

SOUTH AUSTRALIA

road at summit of Stokes Hill, near Wilpena	820 m
Amata–Pipalyatjara Road, Mann Ranges	750 m
Mt Lofty Summit Road, at the summit	726 m
Alligator Gorge Access Road	700 m
Summit Road beneath Mt Lofty	685 m

WESTERN AUSTRALIA

Mt Nameless Road at the summit, near Tom Price	1128 m
Joffre Falls Road west of Mt Vigors	820 m
Juna Downs Station access road	820 m
Mt Bruce Access Road	790 m
Tom Price–Paraburdoo Road south of Tom Price	780 m

TASMANIA

Ben Lomond Summit Road near Legges Tor	1460 m
Mt Barrow Access Road	1340 m
Lake Highway north of Great Lake	1210 m
Poatina Highway east of the Lake Highway	1190 m
Marlborough Highway at Lake Highway junction	1065 m

NORTHERN TERRITORY

Hamilton Downs Access Road west of New Well	840 m
The Garden Station Road near Ankala Hill	820 m
Kintore Road near Liebig Bore	765 m
Stuart Highway near 16 Mile Bore	729 m
Tanami Road east of Mt Everard	725 m

AUSTRALIAN CAPITAL TERRITORY

Mt Ginini Summit Road at the summit	1762 m
Mt Franklin Road	1670 m
Tharwa–Adaminaby Road south of Gudgenby	1400 m
Corin Dam Access Road at Smokers Gap	1250 m
Brindabella Road at Piccadilly Circus	1200 m

TABLE 3.12
HIGHEST RAILWAY IN EACH STATE/TERRITORY

NSW	Blue Cow Mountain Terminal, Skitube Line	1875 m
Vic.	near Millbrook, Western Line	595 m
Qld	north of Ravenshoe, Ravenshoe Line	972 m
SA	near Belalie North, Port Pirie-Peterborough Line	632 m
WA	near Tom Price, Hamersley Line	747 m
Tas.	near Guildford, Emu Bay Line	703 m
NT	at Alice Springs, Central Australian Line	579 m
ACT	near Queanbeyan, Canberra Line	583 m

The Ravenshoe Line, Queensland, though at present officially closed, is still operational, and tourist trains may now be running over this section of track. All other railway lines listed in table 3.12 were operating at the time of writing.

The highest New South Wales railway line used to be on the now-closed Main North Line south of Ben Lomond, Northern Tablelands, at 1376 m above sea level. In Victoria the highest stretches of railway line were on the now-closed and disused Cudgewa Line near Shelley (787 m) and on the Daylesford Line near Bullarto (747m). In Tasmania a disused mining railway south of Rosebery attained an altitude of nearly 800 m. Where the Canberra Line forms a common border with the Australian Capital Territory and New South Wales, it obtains a maximum altitude of approximately 800 m near the Brooks Bank Tunnel.

THE LOWEST RAILWAY IN AUSTRALIA IS ON THE EASTERN SUBURBS RAILWAY BETWEEN CENTRAL AND TOWN HALL, SYDNEY: ELEVATION -13 M.

On the old Ghan Line west of Curdimurka, near Lake Eyre South, the line crossed a creek at an altitude of approximately -10 m.

VOLCANOES AND EARTHQUAKES
Volcanoes

Volcanic activity can raise the level of the land, either by producing distinctive cones or, which is more likely, by issuing lava out of vents. Lava flows bury pre-existing landscapes, forming volcanic plains. If volcanic lavas are particularly viscous, the volcanoes tend to build up into a characteristic tall cone. After the volcano has become extinct and the cone has been subjected to a long period of erosion, all that might remain of it is the erosion-resistant volcanic plug standing high above the surrounding country. Such plugs are often spectacular features and can be seen in the Warrumbungles, New South

Wales, for example, or the Peak Range in central Queensland.

Volcanoes are thought to be extinct in Australia today. The last volcanic activity on the Australian landmass occurred in the Mt Gambier area (Mt Gambier's last eruption was around AD 600) in South Australia. The springs at Paralana in the northern Flinders Ranges, South Australia, where hot water bubbles up to the surface via a fault, give some indication of volcanic activity. Of course, on Heard Island in the Southern Ocean there is an active volcano—Big Ben.

Though in no way a volcanic feature, Australia does have a burning mountain, possibly the oldest and largest of its kind in the world. Near Wingen, New South Wales, there is an underground seam of coal that issues smoke and sulphurous odours through vents in the earth. Giving the illusion of volcanic activity, the fire has been burning for at least 5000 years.

TABLE 3.13
AUSTRALIA'S VOLCANOES

	Last Eruption
ACTIVE	
Big Ben, Heard Island	AD 1992?
POSSIBLY DORMANT	
Mt Gambier, SA	AD 540±90 years
RECENTLY EXTINCT	
Mt Schank, SA	1,400 to 20,000 years ago
Mt Napier, Vic.	1,400 to 20,000 years ago
Mt Eccles, Vic.	1,400 to 20,000 years ago
Tower Hill, Vic.	1,400 to 20,000 years ago
Mt Burr, SA	20,000 years ago
McBride Volcanic Province, Qld	100,000 years ago
ANCIENT	
Mt Canobolas, NSW	11 million years ago
Barrington Tops area, NSW	12 million years ago
Warrumbungles, NSW	16 million years ago
Lord Howe Island/Balls Pyramid, NSW	17 million years ago
Mt Kaputar, Nandewar Range, NSW	18 million years ago
Mt Warning, NSW	21 million years ago
Toowoomba area, Qld	23 million years ago
Glasshouse Mountains, Qld	25 million years ago

Earthquakes

PROBABLY THE MOST EARTHQUAKE-PRONE SETTLEMENT IN AUSTRALIA IS DALTON, ON THE NEW SOUTH WALES SOUTHERN TABLELANDS.

The folding and faulting of the earth's crust (discussed earlier in the section on 'mountain building') usually happens very slowly. But minor adjustments that occur to release the tensions created can result in the rapid movements we experience as earthquakes.

The township of Dalton, New South Wales may well be the settlement most likely to experience earthquakes in Australia. The area around Lake George, nearby to the south, is the centre for many small earthquakes.

THE NORTHERN FLINDERS RANGES, ALONG THE PARALANA FAULT, IN SOUTH AUSTRALIA, IS PROBABLY AUSTRALIA'S MOST EARTHQUAKE-PRONE ZONE.

Along the Paralana fault in the northern Flinders Ranges, very small seismic tremors are experienced almost daily. The sound of the so-called 'rumblings of Arkaroo' heard in the Gammon Ranges, northern Flinders Ranges, is the result of these tremors.

TABLE 3.14
AUSTRALIA'S LARGEST EARTHQUAKES:
BY MAGNITUDE ON THE RICHTER SCALE

YEAR	LOCATION	MAGNITUDE
1941	Meeberrie, north of Geraldton, WA	7.2
1988	Tennant Creek, NT (three major earthquakes)	7.0
1968	Meckering, WA	6.9
1979	Meckering, WA	6.2
1954	Adelaide, SA	5.6
1961	Robertson-Bowral, NSW	5.6
1989	Newcastle, NSW	5.6
1973	Picton, NSW	5.0

Values on the Richter Scale range up to 10 (total devastation). The earthquakes listed in table 3.14 had the potential to cause significant damage to property with resultant loss of life. The extent of these consequences depends on the nearness of inhabited areas and buildings to the centre of the earthquake and on the type of ground beneath them, and whether the buildings are designed to deal with earthquakes. Overall, however, the risk of injury or death caused by earthquakes in Australia is considered to be small.

The Newcastle earthquake was significant in the amount of damage and loss of life it caused. The Tennant Creek earthquake resulted in some people selling up and moving from the town. Interestingly, it used to be thought this area was stable enough to become a site for hazardous wastes. The 1979 Meckering earthquake was significant in that it created a fault 1.5 m wide and 37 km long.

TABLE 3.15
EARTHQUAKE HAZARD POTENTIAL IN AUSTRALIA

1   Meckering/Cadoux districts, WA
2   Furneaux Group, Bass Strait, Tas.
3   Tennant Creek district, NT
4   west of Lake Mackay, Great Sandy Desert, WA
5   parts of the Mt Lofty/Flinders Ranges, SA
6   Hervey Bay district, Qld
7   Poeppels Corner district, Simpson Desert, Qld–SA–NT
8   Lake George–Dalton district, NSW
9   Newcastle district, NSW
10 Millicent district, SA

Table 3.15 lists the risk posed by earthquakes to life and property in a decreasing order of potential hazard.

FOUR

THE LAND: GORGES AND VALLEYS, CAVES AND CRATERS

GORGES AND VALLEYS

Gorges and valleys are generally formed by streams eroding into uplifted land. A valley, usually, is a long depression with fairly regular downward slopes, at the base of which is the stream that has carved the valley from the surface rocks. If you look at a valley in cross-section, you can see its sides are distinguished by hillslopes. These slopes may be very steep (even cliffed) and narrow, thus forming a gorge; or they might be steep but not so narrow, thus forming a canyon, the side tributaries of which are sometimes known as ravines. Small valleys with moderately steep sides are generally known as gullies; particularly attractive ones are sometimes called glens. Valleys mostly tend to be more open than those already described and are common across Australia, but not in plains country. There are many gorges, canyons and gullies on the edges of the higher tablelands.

Moderately steep slopes produce hilly or mountainous country. It is an arbitrary measurement—1000 ft (or approximately 310 m) of local relief—that usually distinguishes a hill from a mountain in definitions. The term 'local relief' refers to the difference in height between a valley's bottom and an adjacent hillslope's summit. Even though Australia has no really high mountains it does have some impressive hillslopes. Mountains are important to some people. Not so long ago the people of Townsville wanted to artificially increase the height of Castle Hill in the centre of the city with quarried material, from 938 ft (286 m), just so that it topped the magic threshold of 1000 ft to become Castle Mountain!

Gentle hillslopes form broad valleys, the stream itself occupying a floodplain in the valley bottom. The slopes may eventually become so gentle that they form peneplains (see chapter 2). A type of valley sometimes found in limestone country is a dry valley, where the stream has disappeared, normally flowing underground through cave systems.

Not all valleys are formed by streams. In areas of faulting (see chapter 3) those parts of the earth's crust that have sunk below the general level of the land form a rift valley. Spencer Gulf and St Vincents Gulf in South Australia occupy rift valleys. In the same type of country where a lowland lies between two uplifted ranges the lowland, itself perhaps uplifted but not as high, is called an intermontane valley or basin. There are such basins in the Flinders Ranges, South Australia.

Deep gorges and valleys

FIGURE 4.1
CROSS-SECTIONS OF SOME AUSTRALIAN VALLEYS AND GORGES

FIGURE 4.2
CROSS-SECTIONS OF THE GREATEST HILLSLOPES IN EACH STATE/TERRITORY

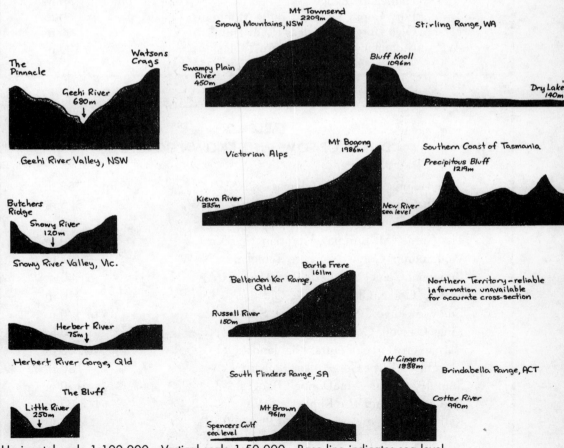

Horizontal scale 1:100,000   Vertical scale 1:50,000   Base line indicates sea level

TABLE 4.1
DEEPEST GORGE IN EACH STATE/TERRITORY

NSW	Kanangra Deep, Blue Mountains	up to 830 m
Vic.	Little River Gorge, Victorian Alps	500 m
Qld	Barron Gorge, Lamb Range	400 m
SA	probably along Alerumba Creek, Flinders Ranges	up to 300 m
WA	unnamed gorge below Mt Frederick, Hamersley Range	345 m
Tas.	Fury Gorge, west of Cradle Mountain	760 m
NT	Olga Gorge, the Olgas (Kata Tjuta)	500 m
ACT	Molonglo Gorge, Southern Tablelands	100 m

TABLE 4.2
DEPTHS OF SOME WELL-KNOWN GORGES

Apsley Gorge, Northern Tablelands, NSW	up to 755 m
Shoalhaven Gorge, Southern Tablelands, NSW	575 m
Hillgrove Gorge, Northern Tablelands, NSW	490 m
The Gorge (Mt Buffalo), Victorian Alps, Vic.	480 m
Wollomombi Gorge, Northern Tablelands, NSW	455 m
Bungonia Gorge, Southern Tablelands, NSW	380 m
Massey Gorge, Clarke Range, Qld	310 m
Ediowie Gorge, Flinders Ranges, SA	up to 300 m
Kings Canyon, George Gill Range, NT	270 m
Carnarvon Gorge, Central Highlands, Qld	200 m
Murchison River Gorge, near Kalbarri, WA	180 m
Standley Chasm, MacDonnell Ranges, NT	150 m
Windjana Gorge, The Kimberley, WA	100 m
Katherine Gorge, Arnhem Land Plateau, NT	60 m

TABLE 4.3
SOME LARGE AND DEEP VALLEYS

Geehi River Valley, Snowy Mountains, NSW	1330 m
Lady Northcotes Canyon, Snowy Mountains, NSW	1000 m
below Frenchmans Cap, The South-West, Tas.	850 m
Snowy River Valley, East Gippsland, Vic.	820 m
Herbert River Gorge, Gorge Range, Qld	610 m
Grose River Valley, Blue Mountains, NSW	600 m
Cotter River Valley, Brindabella Range, ACT	400 m

When is a gorge not a gorge but rather a deep valley? Gorges are usually deep and narrow, which is the reason the canyons of the upper Blue Mountains, New South Wales, have been excluded from table 4.1. Measuring the depth of gorges is fraught with difficulty: while a gorge's bottom is readily determined, its upper levels are often uneven. So, the figures in tables 4.1–4.3 are approximate.

Some of the valleys and gorges mentioned in tables 4.1–4.3 can be seen in cross-section in figure 4.1.

Hillslopes and cliffs

TABLE 4.4
GREATEST HILLSLOPE IN EACH STATE/TERRITORY

NSW	western side of Mt Townsend, Snowy Mountains	1759 m
Vic.	north-western side of Mt Bogong, Victorian Alps	1651 m
Qld	southern side of Mt Bartle Frere, Bellenden Ker Range	1461 m
SA	western side of Mt Brown, Flinders Ranges	961 m
WA	south-eastern side of Bluff Knoll, Stirling Range	956 m
Tas.	western side of Precipitous Bluff, The South-West	1219 m
NT	probably the north-eastern side of Mt Liebig, Amunurunga Range	approx. 900 m
ACT	eastern side of Mt Gingera, Brindabella Range	848 m

The comparative sizes of these hillslopes can be seen from figure 4.2

TABLE 4.5
LONGEST ROAD ASCENT IN EACH STATE/TERRITORY

NSW	Alpine Way, Tom Groggin–Dead Horse Gap, Snowy Mountains	1030 m in 18 km
Vic.	Alpine Road, Harrietville–Mt Hotham, Victorian Alps	1220 m in 29 km
Qld	Gillies Highway, Little Mulgrave–The Bump, Lamb Range	739 m in 17 km
SA	Mt Lofty via Greenhill and Summit Roads, Mt Lofty Ranges	630 m in 9 km
WA	Wittenoom Road, Python Pool to Mt Herbert, Chichester Range	250 m in 12 km
Tas.	North Esk River to Ben Lomond summit	1060 m in 18 km
NT	not applicable	
ACT	Corin Dam Road, Tharwa Rd junction–Smokers Gap, Tidbinbilla Range	580 m in 10 km

Ascents in tables 4.5 and 4.6 are measured as the longest height increase by a single road or railway route up a hillslope; they may also include short downhill sections.

The greatest ascent is not in fact listed here, as it is not totally accessible to the motoring public. Near Swampy Plain Bridge on the Alpine Way there is a section of road to the top of Schlink Pass, north of Guthega, Snowy Mountains, which climbs 1380 m in about 35 km. This road is open to the public as far as Geehi Dam; beyond that it is a Snowy Mountains Authority management road. A place of interest located on this road is Olsens Lookout, which offers awesome views of the Geehi River Valley (Australia's deepest) and the immense hillside of the Main Range beyond (one of Australia's greatest hillslopes).

One of the steepest ascents—as opposed to the longest—is the Jenolan Caves–Oberon Road, Central Tablelands, New South Wales, just west of the caves. This route rises 550 m in 3.3 km, on an average gradient of 1 in 6. Other steep gradient roads include parts of the Maryville–Cumberland Junction Road, Central Highlands, Victoria (with a gradient of 1 in 6); northern access road through the Bunya Mountains National Park, Queensland (also 1 in 6); Sheoak Road, Belair, Mt Lofty Ranges, South Australia (1 in 4.5—probably Australia's steepest road); Seymour Street, Albany, Western Australia (1 in 7.5); Freestone Point Road, Triabunna, Tasmania (1 in 7).

TABLE 4.6
LONGEST RAILWAY ASCENT IN EACH STATE/TERRITORY

NSW	eastern side of the Blue Mountains, Main West Line	990 m in 55.0 km
Vic.	Bacchus Marsh–Ingliston, Western Line	356 m in 21.0 km
Qld	Murphys Creek–Harlaxton, Main Line	396 m in 27.0 km
SA	Clapham–Stirling West, Murray Bridge Line	460 m in 21.0 km
WA	Pinjarra–Dwellingup, Dwellingup Line	254 m in 22.5 km
Tas.	Burnie–Goodwood Siding, Emu Bay Line	600 m in 51.0 km
NT	not applicable	
ACT	not applicable	

The western ascent of the Blue Mountains, New South Wales, between Lithgow and Clarence, rises 138 m in 12 km. While not particularly great in terms of height achieved, the line does pass through 10 tunnels and Australia's deepest railway cutting, and is very scenic. This deviation replaced the famous Zig Zag Railway, a line cut into the side of the mountain in the pattern of a 'Z', the train travelling backwards down the slope of the 'Z'. Tourist trains travel this route today, passing through a tunnel and crossing attractive stone viaducts. Other Australian zig-zags were used to ascend steep hills on the eastern side of the Blue Mountains near Lapstone, and near Kalamunda, Darling Range, Western Australia.

Certainly not the longest railway ascent, the Scenic Railway at Katoomba in the Blue Mountains is, however, by far the steepest. This cable-hauled railway ascends 207 m in 243 m. The steepest gradient on the line is 52° from the horizontal. The Skitube rack railway in the Snowy Mountains, New South Wales, rises 755 m in 8.5 km.

In Victoria the greatest ascent used to be on the Cudgewa Line between Bullioh and Shelley (now disused); it rose 565 m in 30.6 km. In Queensland the Cairns Railway to Kuranda climbs 328 m in 19 km, passing through 15 tunnels and over numerous bridges.

TABLE 4.7
SOME HIGH INLAND CLIFFS AND NEAR-VERTICAL HILLSLOPES

NEW SOUTH WALES
below Watsons Crags, Snowy Mountains	500 m
near Wollomombi Falls, Northern Tablelands	450 m
below Point Lookout, Northern Tablelands	365 m
below Bluff Mountain, Warrumbungle Range	300 m
Kings Tableland, Blue Mountains	295 m
some cliffs in the Blue Mountains	280 m

VICTORIA
Little River Gorge, Victorian Alps	500 m
The gorge below The Chalet, Mt Buffalo	300 m

QUEENSLAND
eastern side of Main Range, Moreton	300 m
near Wallaman Falls, Seaview Range	300 m
below Mt Maroon, Moreton	200 m
Glasshouse Mountains, Moreton	130 m

SOUTH AUSTRALIA
The Gorge, Mt Lofty Ranges	240 m
below St Marys Peak, Flinders Ranges	200 m
some gorges in the Gammon Ranges, Flinders Ranges	150 m

WESTERN AUSTRALIA
below Bluff Knoll, Stirling Range	200 m
some gorges in the Hamersley Range	100 m

TASMANIA
below Frenchmans Cap, The South-West	400 m
below Federation Peak, The South-West	350 m

NORTHERN TERRITORY
within Olga Gorge, the Olgas (Kata Tjuta)	400 m
Jim Jim Creek, Arnhem Land	200 m

AUSTRALIAN CAPITAL TERRITORY
below Booroomba Rocks, Tidbinbilla Range	140 m
above Rendezvous Creek, Tidbinbilla Range	100 m

The heights in table 4.7 are approximate and exclude sea cliffs (covered in chapter 6). Worthy of note, too, are the steep hillslopes of the Great Western Tiers, which rise 1000 m above the bed of the Mersey River in northern Tasmania.

TABLE 4.8
LONGEST CLIFF IN EACH STATE/TERRITORY

NSW	cliffs of the Blue Mountains	280 km
Vic.	coastal cliffs between Princetown and Peterborough	30 km
Qld	probably at Carnarvon Gorge, Central Highlands	30 km
SA	Bunda Cliffs, Nullarbor Plain	210 km
WA	Baxter Cliffs, Nullarbor Plain	165 km
Tas.	cliffs along the east coast of Bruny Island	6 km
NT	cliffs of the Yambarran Range, Victoria River District	over 100 km
ACT	Steamers Beach to Governor Head, Jervis Bay Territory	9 km

It is possible that the discontinuous cliffs bounding the sandstone outcrops of Arnhem Land, Northern Territory, run for many hundreds of kilometres.

THE CLIFFS BELOW FRENCHMANS CAP, TASMANIA, ARE THE HIGHEST SHEER CLIFFS IN AUSTRALIA.

THE GRANITE GORGE BELOW THE CHALET AT MT BUFFALO, VICTORIA, IS CONSIDERED TO BE THE HIGHEST SHEER CLIFF ON THE AUSTRALIAN MAINLAND.

CAVES AND CRATERS

Caves are vacant spaces found on or near the surface of the land. Though not a significant physical feature of the landscape, a cave constitutes an important aspect of people's relationship to the land. Humankind's first home was probably the cave. In the same way that the structure of a building is, a cave is a space not only providing shelter from the elements but, it could be argued, creating an order to its occupier's life.

There are a number of different types of caves. There are rock shelters, which are common in rocky areas. These are formed by overhanging rocks in the base or face of a cliff or by rocks fallen from cliffs or the jumbled tors of granite boulders. Tunnel caves, on the other hand, are created when streams erode weak joint chasms within a band of rock, so forming a cavity (a few rare examples can be found in the sandstone country surrounding Sydney). Lava caves or tunnels are another type, and are fairly common in areas that have experienced lava flows in the past. When the lava cools at different rates, such that some parts continue to flow while other parts have cooled and solidified, then lava caves such as the Undara Lava Tubes in Queensland are formed. Along coastlines sea caves are found, having been formed by wave action eroding weak bands of rock. If a sea cave breaches the surface a short distance inland, blowholes may be formed.

THE COMBINED CLIFF LENGTHS OF THE BAXTER AND BUNDA CLIFFS ALONG THE SOUTHERN EDGE OF THE NULLARBOR PLAIN, TOTAL 375 KM—ONE OF THE LONGEST CONTINUOUS CLIFFLINES IN THE WORLD.

The most familiar caves are limestone caves, which can form within a whole bed of limestone, generally creating the most extensive cave systems and certainly the most complex. In simple terms, the formation of such caves starts when limestone is dissolved in water which contains carbon dioxide derived from the atmosphere and which is slightly acidic. The penetration of this acidic water enlarges minute joints or cracks within the limestone, which eventually causes the rock lying overhead to collapse into the cavity beneath. By this means the cave system grows and can cover many square kilometres and reach great depths. Limestone caves produce a multitude of forms: stalactites (growing down), stalagmites (growing up), sinkholes, collapsed dolines (that is, surfaces collapsing into the cave cavity beneath), underground streams and lakes and large caverns or arch caves. The best known of Australia's limestone caves is probably the Jenolan Caves in New South Wales, while one of the largest limestone belts in the world is found on, and beneath the Nullarbor Plain.

Holes of a different kind are comet and meteorite impact craters. Such extraterrestrial bodies slam into the planet with so great an impact that they produce roughly circular crater depressions surrounded by rims of disturbed earth and rock. Craters and their rims erode over time. Nonetheless, Australia has some superb meteorite craters.

The figure quoted in table 4.9 for the Undara Lava Tubes represents the total length of all passages. The figure for the longest cave takes into account a recent break-through at Jenolan Caves, which occurred at the time of writing and has led speleologists to believe not only that the longest mainland cave would reach 31 km but also that the greatest mainland depth would be exceeded, perhaps reaching over 200 m. As cave exploration is still incomplete, many of the figures in this table may well be exceeded during the lifetime of this book, especially in regard to depth and length.

THE WOLFE CREEK CRATER IS THE SECOND LARGEST METEORITE CRATER IN THE WORLD.

An unusual type of cavern is found on Mt Gee, northern Flinders Ranges, South Australia. Mt Gee is the only crystal quartz mountain in the world and its caverns and grottos are studded with crystal formations.

TABLE 4.9
SIZES OF SOME AUSTRALIAN CAVES

BY LENGTH
longest lava cave   Undara Lava Tubes, Qld   6041m

longest limestone cave
—Australian mainland   Jenolan Caves, NSW   approx. 31 km
—Tasmania   Exit Cave, near Ida Bay   11.8 km

longest single
   limestonenatural shaft   Kellar Cellar, Mt Anne, Tas.   128 m

BY DEPTH
deepest limestone cave
—Australian mainland   Eagles Nest Cave, Yarrongobilly,
                         Snowy Mountains, NSW   174 m
—Tasmania   Growling Swallet, Ice Tube System   378 m
                         Anna-a-Kananda, near Mt Anne   373 m
OTHER
biggest limestone room   Abrakurrie Cave,   335m long,
                         Nullarbor Plain,WA   45 m wide, 30 m high

TABLE 4.10
SOME AUSTRALIAN BIG HOLES

The Bottomless Pit, Jenolan Caves, NSW	149 m
The Big Hole, Duea National Park, NSW	96 m
Devils Coachhouse, Jenolan Caves, NSW	85 m
The Crater, Mt Hypipamee National Park, Qld	58 m
Barrabarrac Hole, Gregory National Park, NT	50 m
Sparkes Gully, Port Campbell district, Vic.	15 m

Since there are many big holes found in limestone country the list in table 4.10 is far from complete. The depth of The Crater, Mt Hypipamee National Park, is to a lake surface; the lake's depth is about 82 m, giving a total depth of 140 m.

Australia's deepest and largest natural holes are related to caves. Big holes are mostly found in limestone cavern country where a part of the roof has collapsed into the cavern beneath. Other big holes are connected with volcanic activity.

It is believed that the craters at Lake Acraman and Gosse Bluff (see table 4.11) were formed by comet impacts. However, it has yet to be confirmed that any supposed comet craters were in fact formed in this way. The remaining four are definitely meteorite impact craters.

TABLE 4.11
AUSTRALIAN METEORITE AND COMET CRATERS

Lake Acraman, Gawler Ranges, SA	1 crater—up to 22 km across
Gosse Bluff, Central Australia, NT	1 crater—4000 m across, 250 m deep
Wolfe Creek Crater, Tanami Desert, WA	1 crater—853 m across, 46 m deep
Henbury Craters, Central Australia, NT	13 craters—largest: 110 m long, 220 m wide, 15 m deep
Boxhole Crater, Central Australia, NT	1 crater—175 m across, 16 m deep
Dalgaranga Crater, Murchison Goldfields, WA	1 crater—21 m across, 3.2 m deep

THE WATER: STREAMS AND WATERFALLS, LAKES AND WETLANDS

STREAMS AND WATERFALLS

Streams

Streams are the basic means of moving water over the surface of the land, and are found throughout much of Australia. The term 'stream' includes what are commonly known as rivers and creeks, though those names can also apply to tidal estuaries. A stream normally contains the water flow in channels; flows operating above the general level of channels are known as floods.

Not all streams flow in channels, however. In some places, particularly in arid Australia, streams flow as sheets across the ground: parts of the upper reaches of the Gascoyne River in Western Australia do this. There are also braided streams, in which a multiplicity of channels intertwine with each other, and they are common in very flat country. The Channel Country of western Queensland is named after the braided channels of the Cooper, Diamantina and Georgina river systems. Another phenomenon associated with flat-country streams is ana-branching: when their channels split and run off as smaller channels, perhaps to rejoin the main stream further on or perhaps even join another river system. An example of ana-branching can be seen in the lower reaches of the Murrumbidgee and Lachlan rivers in the Riverina region of New South Wales.

In Australia many streams are perennial (that is, they flow all year), but most are ephemeral—they only flow after rain. Virtually all arid and semi-arid streams, as well as the tributary creeks in the humid and sub-humid regions are ephemeral. In most cases, however, even ephemeral streams retain water in all but the driest seasons in rockholes and waterholes. Waterholes are also called billabongs and are known as lagoons in northern Australia, pools in Western Australia and holes in Queensland.

Stream channels and their surrounding environs exhibit a number of interesting features. In upland or eroding areas can be seen waterfalls, cataracts, steep-sided gullies, rockholes, rapids, canyons, gorges and bluffs. Downstream, or in areas of deposition, can be found floodplains, meanders, billabongs, terraces, deltas and alluvial fans.

FIGURE 5.1
COMPARATIVE LENGTHS OF AUSTRALIA'S LONGEST RIVERS

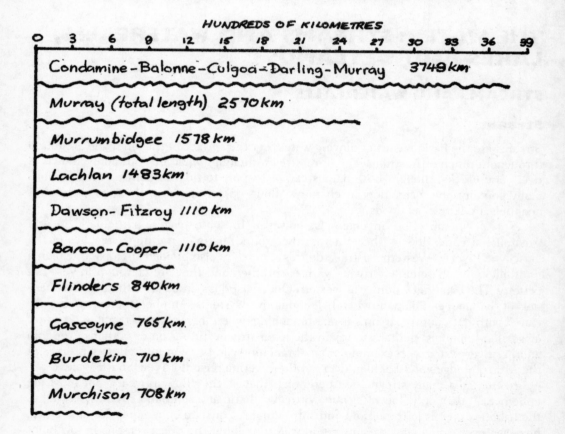

HUNDREDS OF KILOMETRES

Condamine – Balonne – Culgoa – Darling – Murray 3749 km

Murray (total length) 2570 km

Murrumbidgee 1578 km

Lachlan 1483 km

Dawson – Fitzroy 1110 km

Barcoo – Cooper 1110 km

Flinders 840 km

Gascoyne 765 km

Burdekin 710 km

Murchison 708 km

TABLE 5.1
LONGEST RIVERS IN EACH STATE/TERRITORY

NEW SOUTH WALES	
Macintyre–Barwon–Darling–Murray	2771 km
Murray	1936 km
Murrumbidgee	1578 km
Lachlan	1483 km

VICTORIA	
Goulburn	566 km
Glenelg	457 km
Loddon	381 km

QUEENSLAND	
Dawson–Fitzroy	1110 km
Barcoo–Cooper	1110 km
Flinders	840 km
Burdekin	710 km

SOUTH AUSTRALIA	
Murray	642 km
Eateringinna–Alberga–Macumba	630 km
Arckaringa–Neales	400 km

WESTERN AUSTRALIA	
Gascoyne	765 km
Murchison	708 km
Fortescue	547 km

TASMANIA	
South Esk	201 km
Gordon	185 km
Derwent	182 km

NORTHERN TERRITORY	
Victoria	560 km
Roper	418 km
Daly	362 km

AUSTRALIAN CAPITAL TERRITORY	
Naas–Gudgenby–Murrumbidgee	approx. 145 km
Cotter	56 km

AUSTRALIA	
Condamine–Balonne–Culgoa–Darling–Murray	3749 km
Murray (total length)	2570 km

The distances in table 5.1 represent the total length of river channel within each State/Territory. The Murray River has been excluded from Victoria as its southern bank is the northern border of that State. The figures given for the longest rivers in Queensland might well be surpassed by the Torrens–Cornish–Thomson–Cooper system. The total length of the Barcoo–Cooper system in Queensland and South Australia is around 1600 km.

South Australia, the driest State, has very few perennial streams: the longest one to rise within the State is the River Light, 161 km long. Western Australia is mostly dry, too; its longest perennial stream being the Blackwood River, 306 km long. Tasmania has some longish rivers, given the size of the State. If the Tamar Estuary is added to the South Esk River, the total length increases to 271 km.

TABLE 5.2
AUSTRALIA'S LARGEST CATCHMENT AREAS

Murray–Darling, NSW–Vic.–Qld–SA	1,062,530 km²
Cooper, Qld–SA	296,000 km²
Georgina–Eyre, Qld–SA–NT	242,000 km²
Diamantina–Warburton, Qld–SA	158,000 km²
Fitzroy, Qld	142,645 km²
Burdekin, Qld	129,860 km²
Finke, SA–NT	115,000 km²
Flinders, Qld	108,775 km²
Fitzroy, WA	88,980 km²
Murchison, WA	88,000 km²
Roper, NT	81,300 km²
Bulloo, NSW–Qld	78,000 km²
Victoria, NT	77,700 km²
Gascoyne, WA	77,600 km²
Ashburton, WA	76,700 km²

THE COMBINED AREA OF THE LAKE EYRE BASIN IS 1,170,000 KM², MAKING IT THE LARGEST INTERNALLY DRAINED CATCHMENT AREA IN AUSTRALIA. IT IS ALSO CONSIDERED TO BE THE LARGEST PENEPLAIN IN THE WORLD (SEE CHAPTER 2, AND TABLE 2.7).

Catchment areas, sometimes called drainage basins or just basins, are tracts of ground drained by a singular river system. Sometimes the catchment areas that drain into Lake Eyre, South Australia, are considered to be one drainage basin.

Waterfalls

Waterfalls are very scenic and Australia has, surprisingly for such a low and level country, some of the highest waterfalls in the world. This is because most of the rugged upland topography of Australia is created by streams eating away the edges of old tablelands and plateaus.

A waterfall is an interruption in the bed of a stream and is commonly found on the edge of tableland country or where a band of hard rock cuts across the stream bed. There are various types of falls, the best known type being the true falls. This is where water falls over one or more sheer drops, at the base of which is a plunge pool. Lesser known are cataracts or cascades, in which the water flows over a succession of minor drops. But the most common of all are rapids, where the stream flows over and down a bed of large and not-so-large boulders and rocks.

TABLE 5.3
HIGHEST WATERFALL IN EACH STATE/TERRITORY

NSW	Wollomombi Falls, Northern Tablelands—in two drops	488 m
Vic.	Little River Falls, Victorian Alps	245 m
Qld	Wallaman Falls, Seaview Range	278 m
SA	Morialta Falls, Mt Lofty Ranges—in two drops	67 m
WA	Mitchell Falls, The Kimberley	70 m
Tas.	Montezuma Falls, west of Central Plateau	240 m
NT	Jim Jim Falls, Arnhem Land	200 m
ACT	Ginini Falls, Brindabella Range	approx. 25 m

Because waterfalls in South Australia rarely flow, it is hard to measure waterfall heights in that State; consequently, after rain there may be higher falls in the northern Flinders Ranges. The same would be true of Western Australia, where there could be higher falls in the Hamersley Range.

THE HIGHEST SINGLE DROP WATERFALL IN AUSTRALIA IS WALLAMAN FALLS IN QUEENSLAND, WITH A FALL OF 278 M. AFTER HEAVY TROPICAL DOWNPOURS, IT IS AN AWESOME SIGHT.

TABLE 5.4
HEIGHTS OF SOME WELL-KNOWN WATERFALLS

Tully Falls, Tully River, Qld—in more than two drops	300 m
Barron Falls, near Kuranda, Qld	240 m
Apsley Falls, Northern Tablelands, NSW—in two drops	196 m
Wentworth Falls, Blue Mountains, NSW	187 m
Fitzroy Falls, Southern Tablelands, NSW—in two drops	183 m
Bridal Veil Falls, Blue Mountains, NSW	180 m
Katoomba Falls, Blue Mountains, NSW	165 m
Ellensborough Falls, Northern Tablelands, NSW—in a single drop	160 m

LAKES AND WETLANDS

Lakes

Australia is a land of many lakes, an unusual feature in such a dry continent, but less unusual when you consider that most of the lakes are dry. The Aborigines of south-west Queensland could tell whether or not a lake contained water by reading the sky. They were able to do this from a great distance, long before actually seeing the lake itself. A soft lavender-blue rim of haze indicated a large expanse of open country, typically a lake bed. If water is present the rim is brighter, known as *kudje-oobra* or the telling of the water; or if water is not present the rim is darker, called *wir-re-oobra*, the dust shadow. Australia has some of the largest dry lakes in the world—saltlakes (for instance, Lake Eyre, South Australia) and claypans being the most common types. Most saltlakes are covered in a layer of salt and claypans are covered in a fine silt or clay; some dry lakes may have a thin covering of vegetation, however.

Other common lakes are found associated with river systems, such as billabongs (water-holes), or flood-out lakes—for example, Bulloo Lake in north-western New South Wales (some saltlakes are also flood-out lakes). There are also overflow lakes—for instance, the Menindee Lakes in western New South Wales—and back-swamps, which are commonly found on river-ine floodplains. Vegetated back-swamps are perhaps better thought of as wetlands.

Some lakes result from volcanic activity: crater lakes, such as the Blue Lake at Mt Gambier, South Australia; caldera (exploded crater) lakes, such as Tower Hill in western Victoria; maars (depressions intercepting the water table), such as Lake Corangamite, Victoria. Other lakes are formed by glacial action—when ice (or a glacier) deposits debris and rock materials (moraine) and scours the land surface. Cirque lakes such as Blue Lake near Mt Kosciuszko, New South Wales, are glacial lakes occupying ice-scoured depressions; while tarns—Hedley Tarn near Mt Kosciuszko, for instance—are formed by moraines damming creeks

When the water table is intercepted one can find bodies of water. These are common on the coastal plain around Perth during winter; on Fraser Island, Queensland, they are called window lakes. On Fraser Island, too, and in the Great Sandy Region of Queensland there are perched lakes; these are located high on sand dunes and have a bed of impermeable, accumulated organic matter, which holds the water. Coastal dunes obstructing watercourses may form barrage lakes. Other coastal lakes found behind beaches or sand dunes are called lagoons.

Finally, there are the structural lakes, formed by various geological activities: for instance, Lake Karli Tarn, Victoria, created by a landslide damming a stream; or Lake George, New South Wales, which is a good example of a fault-angle lake created by adjacent geological strata. Most unusual are the underground lakes found in limestone country: a lake in Cocklebiddy Cave, Nullarbor Plain, Western Australia, is over 2.5 km long.

TABLE 5.5
AUSTRALIA'S LARGEST NATURAL LAKES

Lake Eyre, SA	9500 km^2
Lake Torrens, SA	5900 km^2
Lake Gairdner, SA	4300 km^2
Lake Mackay, WA–NT	3390 km^2
Lake Frome, SA	2400 km^2
Lake Macleod, WA	2380 km^2
Lake Barlee, WA	1425 km^2
Lake Moore, WA	1160 km^2

The lakes in table 5.5 are all normally dry saltlakes. But Lake Eyre does receive water from time to time and has completely filled a few times over the past century.

Australia's fabled inland sea did actually exist within the past million years or so. Known as Lake Dieri, it covered the region occupied by present-day Lake Eyre and Lake Frome and points inbetween, as well as the basins of the lower Cooper and Strzelecki Creeks and Warburton River. With an approximate surface area of 100,000 km^2, it far exceeded today's largest lakes.

AUSTRALIA'S LONGEST LAKE, AT 270 KM, IS LAKE RAESIDE, NORTH OF KALGOORLIE, WESTERN AUSTRALIA.

TABLE 5.6
LARGEST NATURAL LAKES IN EACH STATE/TERRITORY

NEW SOUTH WALES

Lake Cowal	162 km^2
Lake George	156 km^2
Menindee Lake	155 km^2

VICTORIA

Lake Corangamite	233 km^2
Lake Tyrrell	172 km^2
Lake Hindmarsh	121 km^2

QUEENSLAND

Lake Yamma Yamma	712 km^2
Lake Philippi	326 km^2
Lake Machattie	310 km^2

SOUTH AUSTRALIA

Lake Eyre	9500 km^2
Lake Torrens	5900 km^2
Lake Gairdner	4300 km^2

WESTERN AUSTRALIA

Lake Macleod	2380 km^2
Lake Barlee	1425 km^2
Lake Moore	1160 km^2

TASMANIA

Great Lake	115 km^2
Lake Sorell	49 km^2
Lake St Clair	38 km^2

NORTHERN TERRITORY

Lake Amadeus	880 km^2
Lake Woods	area varies
Lake Sylvestor	area varies

AUSTRALIAN CAPITAL TERRITORY

Lake Windermere, Jervis Bay Territory	approx. 0.4 km^2

FIGURE 5.2
COMPARATIVE SIZES OF THE LARGEST LAKES IN EACH STATE/TERRITORY

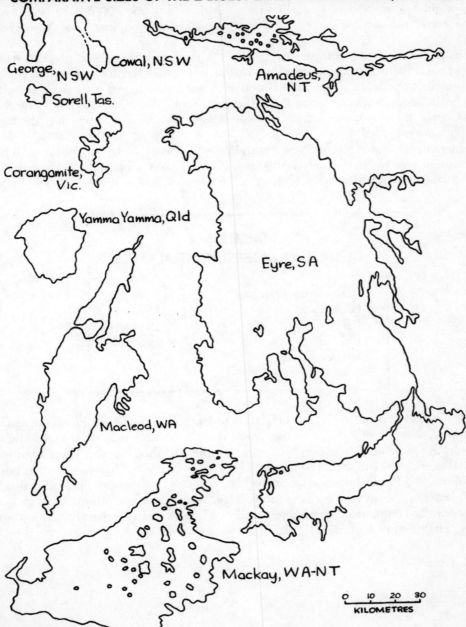

Coastal lagoons are not taken into account in the compilation of table 5.6. The sizes given in this table for Menindee Lake, New South Wales, and Great Lake, Tasmania, are their original size before alteration for hydrological works. The lake sizes given for Western Australia are exceeded by the large, border-straddling Lake Mackay (see table 5.5).

Figure 5.2 shows the comparative sizes of the largest (as they are at present) natural lakes of each State/Territory, except the Australian Capital Territory, for which the lake is too small at this scale. Thus, Lake Sorell is shown for Tasmania because of the effect of the hydrological works on Great Lake. For New South Wales, as both Lake Cowal and Lake George are almost the same size, there is some question as to which is the larger; thus both are included.

The figures in table 5.6 for New South Wales are exceeded by the outline of a huge lake with an area of approximately 500 km². Called Lake Garnpung, it is the bed of an ancient lake system which flowed from the prehistoric Lachlan River.

TABLE 5.7
AUSTRALIA'S HIGHEST NATURAL LAKES

Lake Cootapatamba	2050 m
Club Lake	1950 m
Lake Albina	1915 m
Blue Lake	1900 m
Hedley Tarn	1860 m

All the lakes in table 5.7 are of glacial origin and situated in the vicinity of Mt Kosciuszko, New South Wales, where there are also some smaller unnamed lakes or pools. In the same area, between Mt Townsend and Mt Alice Rawson, there used to be a glacial lake called Russel Tarn or Lake Claire. This lake was situated at an altitude of approximately 2150 m but now seems to have completely dried up. Tasmania also has many glacial lakes, situated on its central plateau at an altitude of above 1000 m.

By way of comparison, the highest artificial lake is Pretty Valley Pondage, on the Bogong High Plains, Victoria, at 1630 m above sea level.

TABLE 5.8
HIGHEST NATURAL LAKE IN EACH STATE/TERRITORY

NSW	Lake Cootapatamba, Snowy Mountains	2050 m
Vic.	Lake Karli Tarn, Victorian Alps	914 m
Qld	Lake Eacham, Atherton Tableland	755 m
SA	Lake Wilson, Mann Ranges	680 m
WA	Lakes Edith-Whitnel and Karri Karri, Murchison Goldfields	approx. 610 m
Tas.	Menamatta Tarns, Ben Lomond Plateau	1430 m
NT	Lake Lewis, south of Yuendumu	552 m
ACT	not applicable	

South Australia's highest permanent lake is Silver Lake, Mt Lofty Ranges, at a height of 290 m.

The listing in table 5.8 is probably not complete. Apart from the dried-up Russel Tarn in the Snowy Mountains, New South Wales (see the comments to table 5.7, above), in Tasmania, beneath the summit of Mt Ossa, there is a small pool-sized tarn at an approximate height of 1610 m. Near the Irriki Range in central Australia there are claypans lying at an estimated 670 m above sea level. In Western Australia it is possible that Lake Kerrylyn, north of Mt Methwin, on the edge of the Little Sandy Desert, may be higher than the one listed for that State.

TABLE 5.9
SOME LAKE DEPTHS

Lake St Clair, Tas.	168 m
Blue Lake, SA	75 m
Lake Eacham, Qld	70 m
Lake Bullenmerri, Vic.	62 m
Lake Barrine, Qld	60 m

The lakes in table 5.9 are probably representative of Australia's deepest lakes but the list is far from complete. Interestingly, the four shallower lakes are of volcanic origin while Lake St Clair, Australia's deepest lake, is of glacial origin. One reference has Lake St Clair's depth measured at 200 m. Near Wyndham, Western Australia, is The Grotto, a deep rockhole; one measurement of its depth is over 120 m, even though its surface area is about the size of a suburban house.

Wetlands

Wetlands are tracts of countryside subjected to permanent, seasonal or irregular inundation and can be one of two basic types: freshwater or marine. Wetlands, once despised as marshes and swamps, are important aquatic habitats supporting a vast range of plant and animal life. In fact, they are normally characterised by the vegetation they support; in this respect they are different to lakes.

Numerous types of freshwater wetlands are found throughout Australia, especially in the humid and sub-humid country of eastern and south-western Australia or in the monsoonal north. Examples of freshwater wetlands include: rivers and river flats; creeks and creek margins; various herb, sedge, lignum and canegrass swamps; button-grass plains; reed and shrub marshes; wet heaths; and open bodies of water containing aquatic plants. As well, though not necessarily 'freshwater', there are saltlakes and hypersaline lakes.

Marine wetlands, being coastal, include such types as tidal estuaries, mangrove formations, coastal lagoons, salt marshes. Their defining feature is salty or brackish water, which obviously influences the types of vegetation found in these wetlands.

TABLE 5.10
SOME AUSTRALIAN WETLANDS

Kakadu Wetlands, NT	300,000 ha	
Macquarie Marshes, NSW	95,000 ha	(190,000 ha)
Lowbidgee Wetlands, Riverina, NSW	20,000 ha	(40,000 ha)
Coongie Lakes, Strzelecki Desert, SA	7,730 ha	
Gwydir Wetlands, NSW	5,000 ha	(27,000 ha)
Bool/Hack Lagoons, SA	3,600 ha	

In table 5.10 the figures in brackets are the original sizes of those wetlands before human interference. Extraction for irrigation farming has led to significant reductions in the streams that feed these wetlands.

Obviously there are many other wetlands around Australia and this list is far from complete. Other major wetlands include the coastal country around the Gulf of Carpentaria, the wetlands of Lakeland National Park in far north Queensland, the Townsville area of north Queensland, the Moreton Bay region of southern Queensland, the coastal plains south of Perth, Western Australia, and the 'button-grass plains' of south-west Tasmania.

OTHER WATER FEATURES

TABLE 5.11
SOME AUSTRALIAN HOT SPRINGS

Yarrangobilly, Snowy Mountains, NSW	27°C
Innot, near Mt Garnet, Qld	80°C
Tallaroo, west of Mt Surprise, Qld	92°C
Paralana, Flinders Ranges, SA	95°C
Dalhousie, north of Oodnadatta, SA	43°C
Blanche Cup, near Lake Eyre South, SA	approx. 25°C
The Bubbler, near Lake Eyre South, SA	approx. 25°C
Zebedee, The Kimberley, WA	25°C
Mataranka, Top End, NT	31°C
Douglas, Top End, NT	60°C

The figures in table 5.11 represent typical temperatures of spring waters either at point of issue or in nearby bathing facilities, and are approximate.

The hot springs listed here are naturally occurring and should not be confused with artesian bores. Hot spring waters emanate from within the earth's crust, where they have been heated. The origin of the heat may be volcanic (as, for example, at Tallaroo or Paralana) or it may simply be that the spring's source lies deep enough within the earth's crust (for example, Dalhousie).

The main Dalhousie hot spring is interesting inasmuch as it is just one of around 80 springs in the vicinity. The Dalhousie Springs are natural outlets of the Great Artesian Basin (see comments beneath table 5.12), as are Blanche Cup and The Bubbler. These natural artesian springs are sometimes known as mound springs. This is because the sediment particles which their waters carry to the surface, together with chemical precipitates, create mounds that are often quite a few metres high. Typically, the water flows from the top or sides of these mounds. There are at least 90 mound springs, or complexes of springs, in South Australia alone. Many mounds are relict springs, having dried up in the past.

Not all Great Artesian Basin springs flow with water. Near Eulo in south-west Queensland, and elsewhere, there are mud springs. These are mounds of dried mud; occasionally, when the underlying pressure becomes too great, they blow their tops.

TABLE 5.12
SOME HYDROLOGICAL WORKS

Highest Dam Walls	
—Dartmouth Dam, Victorian Alps, Vic.	180 m
—Talbingo Dam, Snowy Mountains, NSW	161 m
Longest Dam Wall	
—Ross River Dam, Burdekin Basin, Qld	8168 m
Deepest Bore	
—Springleigh Bore, Great Artesian Basin, Qld	2136 m
Longest Single Hydro-Scheme Tunnel	
—Eucumbene–Snowy, Snowy Mountains, NSW	23.4 km
Longest Linked Hydro-Scheme Tunnel	
—Eucumbene–Snowy/Snowy–Geehi/Murray	
One Pressure Tunnel, Snowy Mountains, NSW	49.7 km

The Great Artesian Basin is a geological feature in which water is held under pressure in spaces (aquifers) within layers of sandstone deep below the surface. It covers 1.74 million km^2 of New South Wales, Queensland and South Australia, and currently has approximately 3100 active artesian bores (down from a maximum of 4700). The bores are used for stock watering, mining and domestic purposes. There are two types of bores: artesian and sub-artesian. Artesian bores flow naturally without the assistance of pumping; in sub-artesian bores the water is pumped to the surface, usually by windmills. There are approximately 20,000 sub-artesian bores in the Great Artesian Basin. It has been estimated that only about 10 per cent of the bore water is effectively used.

Lake Argyle, in The Kimberley, Western Australia, which floods over 700 km^2 of countryside, has the largest area of any reservoir. There are approximately 342 major dams and reservoirs in Australia.

THE COAST

THE COASTLINE

Most Australians are familiar with coasts because most Australians live near one—in fact, about three out of four people live within an hour's drive of the sea. Around nine out of ten people live within 50 km of the coast on a strip extending from Port Douglas in Queensland to Ceduna in South Australia and around the south-west corner of Western Australia.

While extensive bays and gulfs form the shape of the coastline, along the shores of Australia there are a number of different types of coasts to be found—such as beach coasts, rock coasts, tidal plain coasts or, off parts of the tropical coast, coral reefs and sandy cays. The most unusual Australian coast, however, occurs on Heard Island in the Southern Ocean. Here active glaciers have snouts which override the land surface to form ice coasts.

TABLE 6.1
COASTLINE LENGTH FOR EACH STATE/TERRITORY

NSW	1,900 km
Vic.	1,800 km
Qld	7,400 km
SA	3,700 km
WA	12,500 km
Tas.	3,200 km
NT	6,200 km
ACT	35 km
AUSTRALIA	36,735 km

There is some confusion over the length of the Australian coastline. The figure given in table 6.1 is quoted from the *Year Book Australia*, but other sources give different figures. A CSIRO study found that the length of coastline was 30,270 km including Tasmania, and 47,070 km if all islands are included; the *Australian Handbook* quotes 19,320 km and the *Australian Encyclopaedia,* 19,650 km. The different figures are due to different techniques in measuring coastlines—whether or not bays, estuaries or islands are included for instance.

Gulfs and bays

Embayments are indentations in the coastline. Bays are usually thought of as indentations of the land by bodies of water, in this case the sea or ocean. Gulfs are generally large embayments that penetrate far into the land. They are formed either by rising sea levels flooding plains—for instance, the Gulf of Carpentaria; or by faults in the earth's crust resulting in a rift valley that is consequently flooded by the sea—for instance, Spencer Gulf and St Vincent Gulf.

AUSTRALIA'S MOST EXTENSIVELY BAYED COAST IS THE KIMBERLEY COAST OF WESTERN AUSTRALIA.

Along the Kimberley Coast numerous valleys have been flooded by rising sea levels since the last ice age; this has resulted in the creation of many bays, gulfs and numerous off-shore islands, a number of which form the Buccaneer and Bonaparte archipelagoes.

The figures in table 6.2 are approximate, for there is no specific boundary to an embayment. Although some of these places are named 'sound', they would perhaps be better termed bays or gulfs, since a sound is really a narrow water passage, like a strait.

Beach coasts

Beach coasts have lengthy beaches, behind which there is usually a complex of dunes with perhaps minor features such as estuaries and lagoons—for instance, sections of the north coast of New South Wales. There is also a special type of beach coast, called a barrier beach coast, which has the lengthy beaches and dune complexes but is separated from the mainland by extensive lagoon systems—such as in the Gippsland Lakes district of Victoria or along The Coorong of South Australia.

Lagoons are coastal lakes partly or totally separated from the sea by narrow strips of land. This land could be sand spits, sandhills or, in the case of submerged coasts, low-lying hills or ridges. Lagoons, if connected to the sea, will be tidal; their waters may be salty, brackish or fresh.

Beaches are largely formed by wave action, and some are gently curved, making a concave shape with the shoreline. Beaches are generally composed of sand-sized particles with a range of colour variation that is dependent on the constituent minerals of the sands. The sands can range in colour from nearly white, common in the south-west of

```
┌──────────────────────────────────────────────────┐
│                                                    │
│                    TABLE 6.2                       │
│       SOME AUSTRALIAN GULFS AND EMBAYMENTS:        │
│                    BY AREA                         │
│                                                    │
│   Gulf of Carpentaria, Qld–NT        335,000 km²   │
│   Joseph Bonaparte Gulf, WA–NT        58,000 km²   │
│   Spencer Gulf, SA                    20,000 km²   │
│   Shark Bay, WA                       16,500 km²   │
│   Van Diemen Gulf, NT                 11,500 km²   │
│   King Sound, WA                       8,200 km²   │
│   St Vincent Gulf, SA                  5,200 km²   │
│   Hervey Bay, Qld                      4,500 km²   │
│   Exmouth Gulf, WA                     4,200 km²   │
│   Moreton Bay, Qld                     3,300 km²   │
│   Admiralty Gulf, WA                   2,700 km²   │
│   Broad Sound, Qld                     2,700 km²   │
│   Port Phillip Bay, Vic.               1,950 km²   │
│   Blue Mud Bay, NT                     1,800 km²   │
│   Shoalwater Bay, Qld                  1,300 km²   │
│   Oyster Bay, Tas.                       600 km²   │
│   Roebuck Bay, WA                        600 km²   │
│   York Sound, WA                         500 km²   │
│   Port Jackson, Sydney, NSW               55 km²   │
│   Botany Bay, Sydney, NSW                 50 km²   │
│                                                    │
└──────────────────────────────────────────────────┘
```

TABLE 6.2
SOME AUSTRALIAN GULFS AND EMBAYMENTS: BY AREA

Gulf of Carpentaria, Qld–NT	335,000 km^2
Joseph Bonaparte Gulf, WA–NT	58,000 km^2
Spencer Gulf, SA	20,000 km^2
Shark Bay, WA	16,500 km^2
Van Diemen Gulf, NT	11,500 km^2
King Sound, WA	8,200 km^2
St Vincent Gulf, SA	5,200 km^2
Hervey Bay, Qld	4,500 km^2
Exmouth Gulf, WA	4,200 km^2
Moreton Bay, Qld	3,300 km^2
Admiralty Gulf, WA	2,700 km^2
Broad Sound, Qld	2,700 km^2
Port Phillip Bay, Vic.	1,950 km^2
Blue Mud Bay, NT	1,800 km^2
Shoalwater Bay, Qld	1,300 km^2
Oyster Bay, Tas.	600 km^2
Roebuck Bay, WA	600 km^2
York Sound, WA	500 km^2
Port Jackson, Sydney, NSW	55 km^2
Botany Bay, Sydney, NSW	50 km^2

Western Australia (though the whitest beach sands are said to be at Hyams Beach, Jervis Bay, New South Wales) through to deep yellow, common on the east coast of Australia.

Not all beaches are sandy. Shingle beaches, composed of pebble-sized particles, are rare in Australia, however. Pebbly Beach, on the New South Wales south coast, is a good example. At Shark Bay, Western Australia, there is the aptly named Shell Beach, composed of innumerable mollusc shells. In another type of beach, those fronting shores with high tidal ranges, broad foreshores of mud are revealed at low tide. Shallow temporary lagoons often form on these tidal flats as the tide ebbs. Such beach coasts can be seen at Western Port, Victoria, and in Edgecombe Bay near Bowen, north Queensland and around Port Hedland in Western Australia.

Coupled with beach and barrier beach coasts there are various distinctive landforms. Spits, for instance, are common. A spit is created when a tongue of sand (and sometimes silt or even pebbles) is formed by waves and currents, so extending the beach into a small point that projects into a bay or the sea—the northern tip of Fraser Island, Queensland, is a good example. The longest elongated spit or silt jetty is 9.7 km; it is located where the Mitchell River enters Lake King, one of the interconnected Gippsland Lakes, Victoria.

A spit that connects a rocky off-shore island to the mainland is called a tombolo—Barrenjoey, north of Palm Beach at the mouth of the Hawkesbury River, New South Wales, is one example. In some places spits may enclose bodies of water, so forming coastal lagoons.

Behind most beaches there are sand dunes—massive mounts of sand that usually lie parallel to the shoreline with a depression (or swale) separating each successive dune. On Fraser Island, Queensland, the tallest sand dunes reach a height of 240 m. Mt Tempest, on Moreton Island, Queensland, which is 280 m high, is considered to be the highest sand dune in Australia.

The dune nearest the coast (the foredune) often acts as a sand reservoir during storms and tempests, when beach sands may be eroded and deposited off-shore as bars. If stabilising dune vegetation is disturbed, then the sand is subjected to winds which may form blow-outs. Extensive blow-outs may produce large areas of jumbled and drifting sand dunes called sand patches. The Delisser Sandhills at Eucla, Nullarbor Plain, Western Australia, were formed by rabbits denuding the dunes' protective cover of vegetation.

TABLE 6.3
LONGEST BEACH IN EACH STATE/TERRITORY

NSW	Newcastle Bight Beach, north of Stockton	30 km
Vic.	Ninety-Mile Beach, Gippsland	145 km
Qld	Seventy-Five-Mile Beach, Fraser Island	120 km
SA	Younghusband Peninsula/Lacepede Beach, The Coorong	175 km
WA	Eighty-Mile Beach, Great Sandy Desert	175 km
Tas.	Ocean Beach, near Strahan	34 km
NT	Aurari Bay Beach, Arnhem Land	17 km
ACT	Bherwerre Beach, Jervis Bay Territory	5 km

Aurari Bay Beach, in table 6.3, may not be the longest beach in the Northern Territory. As a point of interest, Eighty-Mile Beach, Western Australia, should be called One-Hundred-and-Ten-Mile Beach.

TABLE 6.4
LARGEST LAGOON IN EACH STATE/TERRITORY

NSW	Lake Macquarie	115.0 km²
Vic.	Gippsland Lakes	380.0 km²
Qld	Noosa Lakes	60.0 km²
SA	Lakes Alexandrina–Albert–Coorong	970.0 km²
WA	Peel–Harvey Inlet, near Mandurah	130.0 km²
Tas.	Moulting Lagoon, near Swansea	50.0 km²
NT	unknown	
ACT	lagoon east of Naval College, Jervis Bay Territory	0.1 km²

LAKE MACQUARIE IS OFTEN CITED AS AUSTRALIA'S LARGEST LAGOON; IT CERTAINLY IS THE LARGEST SINGULAR LAGOON BODY OF WATER WITH ONE NAME.

In table 6.4 the sizes of the lagoons are approximate. Some of the lagoons named there are two or more lagoons joined by narrow waterways. These lagoons exclude coral lagoons or those inland waterholes called lagoons in northern Australia.

Rock coasts

Another type of coast is the rock coast, which is characterised by low or high rocky cliffs. They may have small beaches at the base of the cliffs or lying between successive headlands.

Sea levels rose to their present height about 6000 years ago, and so waves have been eroding cliffs at their base for this length of time. Depending on the resistance of the rock, various features may be formed. Very hard rocks form plunging cliffs and headlands or, in the case of granite domes, steeply sloping rock surfaces upon which king waves occasionally wash up the rock's surface and whisk away unaware fisherfolk. The sloping granite dome of Rodondo Island, Bass Strait, for example, which is visible from Wilsons Promontory in Victoria, rises 350 m above sea level.

Normally, though, rock coasts exhibit rock platforms—flat expanses of rock generally situated between the high and low tide levels. Rock platforms are fascinating places to view the marine life that lives in or near rockpools, or has been left stranded by ebbing tides.

Rock coasts composed of readily eroding rocks also exhibit many erosional features such as stacks (isolated pillars of rock), blowholes, sea caves and sea gorges. The Port Campbell coast of western Victoria has excellent examples of all of these features.

Another feature found on such coasts is sea arches. Tasman Arch on Tasman Peninsula, Tasmania, at 52 m, is probably Australia's highest sea arch.

TABLE 6.5
HIGHEST SEA-CLIFFS IN EACH STATE/TERRITORY

NSW	below Mt Gower, Lord Howe Island	770 m
Vic.	cliffs near The Twelve Apostles, Port Campbell district	60–100 m
Qld	probably Indian Head, Fraser Island	120 m
SA	Cape Torrens, Kangaroo Island	220 m
WA	Zuytdorp Cliffs, south of Shark Bay	250 m
Tas.	Cape Pillar, Tasman Peninsula	275 m
NT	Rainbow Cliffs, Arnhem Land	50 m
ACT	Steamers Head, Jervis Bay Territory	135 m

The figures in table 6.5 represent sheer cliffs and may not be complete. Balls Pyramid, part of the Lord Howe Island Group, rises 558 m sheer out of the water. The sandstone cliffs at Garie, south of Sydney, New South Wales, are 120 m high.

It is worth noting that the Zuytdorp Cliffs, Western Australia, are 130 km in length. And the cliffs at Cape Pillar, Tasmania, extend for another 275 m below sea level, giving a total fall of 550 m.

Tidal plain coasts

Very flat coasts with vast tidal plains which are regularly or seasonally inundated are called tidal plain coasts. These are are coasts where the land is forming at the expense of the sea. Found in areas of still waters, they are dominated by mudflats, salt marshes, mangrove formations and estuaries. Good examples can be seen at Corner Inlet, Victoria, or the southern coast of the Gulf of Carpentaria.

TIDES

The alternate rising and fall of the sea—the tides—is caused by the gravitational pull of the moon and the sun. Tides usually occur twice a day, but south of Geraldton, Western Australia, there is only one tide (high or low) a day. At Hamelin Pool in Shark Bay, Western Australia, the tides are barely discernible.

The largest tides are the spring tides, which occur when the earth, sun and moon are in a line. The gravitational pull of the sun and moon being at their greatest at this time, this makes for higher high tides and lower low tides. When the earth is closest to the sun (around January), these effects are even greater. The converse of a spring tide—called a neap tide—occurs when the sun and moon are at right angles to each other. Then, they partly cancel out each other's tidal influence, which results in lower high tides and higher low tides. Spring and neap tides occur twice a month.

The most interesting tidal activity happens in Western Australia, where the greatest and least tidal ranges are (see table 6.6). Where tidal ranges are great, long piers must be built for ships to anchor at low water. It is not uncommon to see small boats sitting on the bottom at low tide in these places. Tidal ranges vary for many reasons, including shallowness of water, constrictions in estuaries, and so on. Rock coasts with great tidal ranges can exhibit tidal waterfalls. Ebbing and flooding tides entering or leaving constricted inlets have different water levels, thus producing a waterfall.

Tidal bores are wave-like features, in which the oversteep wave of the tidal front produces a surf. Tidal race indicates the speed of a tide. In deep water this is approximately 1 km/hr and in shallow water, up to 7 km/hr; these speeds being faster in constricted areas.

TABLE 6.6
TIDES

SPRING TIDAL RANGES
Least
—south of Perth, WA   up to 60 cms
Greatest
—Collier Bay, The Kimberley, WA   10.97 m
—Derby, The Kimberley, WA   10.36 m
—Broome, The Kimberley, WA   8.53 m
—different sites in Broad Sound, Qld   7.31 to 9.14 m
—Wyndham, The Kimberley, WA   7.01 m

LONGEST TIDAL BORE
—up the Victoria River, NT   80 km

TIDAL RACES
—The Rip, Port Phillip Heads, Vic.   up to 14.4 km/hr
—Wyndham, The Kimberley, WA   up to 17.0 km/hr
—Walcott Inlet, The Kimberley, WA   up to 28.0 km/hr

TABLE 6.7
SPRING TIDAL RANGES IN THE CAPITAL CITIES

NSW	Sydney, Fort Denison	1.2 m
Vic.	Melbourne, Williamstown	0.8 m
Qld	Brisbane, Brisbane Bar	1.9 m
SA	Adelaide, Port Adelaide	2.0 m
WA	Perth, Fremantle	0.7 m
Tas.	Hobart, Derwent River	1.3 m
NT	Darwin, Port Darwin	5.6 m

The figures in table 6.7 represent average high- and low-water spring tidal ranges.

OFF-SHORE
Australia's islands, reefs and straits

TABLE 6.8
THE NUMBER OF AUSTRALIA'S ISLANDS

STATES/TERRITORIES	
NSW	40
Vic.	80
Qld	1000
SA	140
WA	320
Tas.	110
NT	110
ACT	1
OCEANIC ISLANDS	
Pacific Ocean	4
Southern Ocean	4
Indian Ocean	5
AUSTRALIA (total)	1810

The number of islands is approximate; included is just about everything from barely exposed mud and sand banks to rocky islets and large landmasses separated from the mainland by narrow straits. All different types of islands are included for table 6.8—estuarine, continental and oceanic islands, and coral formations.

The islands associated with the States/Territories are mostly continental islands. In other words, they were formed as a result of being separated from the mainland by rising sea levels after the last ice age—the islands themselves being the summits of ancient hills or mountains. Some of the Queensland islands are coral islands formed and built up by coral polyps. The oceanic islands were formed independently of the mainland and are either volcanic or coral islands.

TABLE 6.9
AUSTRALIA'S LARGEST ISLANDS

Tasmania	6,780,000 ha
Melville Island, Arafura Sea, NT	621,320 ha
Kangaroo Island, Southern Ocean, SA	434,920 ha
Groote Eylandt, Gulf of Carpentaria, NT	245,940 ha
Flinders Island, Bass Strait, Tas.	161,800 ha
Bathurst Island, Arafura Sea, NT	153,320 ha
Mornington Island, Gulf of Carpentaria, Qld	88,020 ha
King Island, Bass Strait, Tas.	82,905 ha
Dirk Hartog Island, Shark Bay, WA	61,890 ha
Hinchinbrook Island, Coral Sea, Qld	39,350 ha
Cape Barren Island, Bass Strait, Tas.	33,530 ha

TABLE 6.10
LARGEST ISLAND IN EACH STATE/TERRITORY

NSW	Broughton Island, Tasman Sea	463 ha
Vic.	French Island, Western Port Bay	16,705 ha
Qld	Mornington Island, Gulf of Carpentaria	88,020 ha
SA	Kangaroo Island, Southern Ocean	434,920 ha
WA	Dirk Hartog Island, Shark Bay	61,890 ha
Tas.	Flinders Island, Bass Strait	161,800 ha
NT	Melville Island, Arafura Sea	621,320 ha
ACT	Bowen Island, Jervis Bay	53 ha

By way of contrast, near Camperdown in Victoria's Western Districts there are floating islands on a small lake. These islands, up to 30 m across, are composed of peat and support vegetation up to 8 m high. The vegetation acts as a sail and the wind blows the islands across the lake's surface.

TABLE 6.11
CORAL REEFS

Great Barrier Reef, Coral Sea	2300 km
Ningaloo Reef, Indian Ocean	250 km
Houtman Abrolhos, Indian Ocean	80 km

The figures in table 6.11 for the coral reefs represent total lengths.

Coral coasts are common off central and northern Queensland and the Exmouth Peninsula of Western Australia, and can be found along parts of the tropical coastline.

The Great Barrier Reef is in fact composed of up to 3400 individual reefs ranging in size from a few thousand square metres up to 120 km^2; the width of combined reefs ranges up to 250 km. The Houtman Abrolhos reefs are the largest most southerly coral reefs in the world.

TABLE 6.12
LENGTHS OF SOME AUSTRALIAN STRAITS

Bass Strait	off northern Tasmania	350 km
Torres Strait	off northern Queensland	320 km
Investigator Strait	off Yorke Peninsula, SA	125 km
Apsley Strait	between Melville and Bathurst Islands, NT	75 km
Great Sandy Strait	between the mainland and Fraser Island, Qld	75 km
Sunday Strait	off Dampier Land, WA	65 km
Cadell Strait	off Arnhem Land, NT	60 km
Dundas Strait	off Cobourg Peninsula, NT	50 km
Endeavour Strait	off Cape York Peninsula, Qld	45 km
Banks Strait	off north-eastern Tasmania	40 km
Clarence Strait	between the mainland and Melville Island, NT	35 km

---

THE COAST

The lengths in table 6.12, although approximate, are indicative of the longest stretches of water off Australia's coastline which bear the name 'strait'.

A strait is a narrow stretch of sea connecting two broad expanses of sea. Sometimes straits are called passages or channels—for example, the Whitsunday Passage, or the D'Entrecasteaux Channel. Similarly, a sound is really a narrow passage like a strait.

There are also, of course, some extensive passages and channels. For instance, there is the unfortunately named Backstairs Passage (approximately 65 km), off Fleurieu Peninsula, South Australia; the Whitsunday Passage (approximately 70 km), Central Queensland Coast-Whitsunday Group, Queensland; D'Entrecasteaux Channel (approximately 65 kilometres), between Bruny Island and mainland Tasmania.

THE DEEPEST OCEAN TRENCH NEAR THE AUSTRALIAN MAINLAND, THE DIAMANTINA, LIES OFF POINT D'ENTRECASTEAUX, WESTERN AUSTRALIA, AT A DEPTH OF 6100 M.

89

SEVEN

THE BUSH

The vegetated countryside, at first glance, presents a bewildering array of living matter. Its life forms vary from district to district—sometimes dramatically, more usually subtly. Depending on rock type, topography, various weather phenomena, fires, soils, and the influence of animal and human activity, vegetation produces different types of what are called formations. On a large scale these plant formations roughly parallel climatic regions. On a smaller scale the prevailing rock type, together with the slope of the land and the direction it faces, all combine with soils to produce variations within these larger formations.

Nevertheless, the many different types of vegetation formations do exhibit a general trend towards uniformity in their appearance. Consequently, to a traveller in a speeding car the vegetation appears as a hodge-podge of trunks, leaves, shrubs and grasses—seemingly without form. This is why the vegetated countryside is often perceived as boring: forest trees block the view, mallee scrubs are tedious to traverse, and saltbush-covered plains make one feel very small or an insignificant part of the landscape. But the countryside does not have to be perceived in this way.

It is possible to view vegetation systematically. Although no classification is perfect, owing to the complexity of variables involved, one particular formation can be differentiated from another simply by looking at how each one is composed. One common system of differentiation used in Australia is based on the dominant type of vegetation (that is, tree, shrub or herb), its height above the ground, and the 'ground area' covered by its foliage, which is known as its projective foliage cover.

With the use of this classification system, vegetation can be grouped into various formations, such as different types of forest, woodland, scrub, heath, shrubland and herbland. Other formations do not fit so readily into this classification because they occupy extreme habitats such as tidal flats, wetlands, or sand dunes. The most common of these other types include mangrove formations, the incredible diversity of wetlands, the plant life on coastal sand dunes and, off-shore, seagrass formations. By way of interest, Australia's largest seagrass formation, the Wooramel seagrass bank, grows in Shark Bay, Western Australia, and covers 1000 km^2.

TYPES OF VEGETATION

TABLE 7.1
AUSTRALIA'S VEGETATION FORMATIONS: PRE-1788

FORMATION	AREA OCCUPIED (M=million)	TYPICAL PLANT TYPES
Shrublands	3.07M km^2	mulga and other acacias, mallee eucalypts
Woodlands	2.18M km^2	various eucalypts
Herblands	0.59M km^2	Mitchell grass
Open scrubs	0.59M km^2	mallee eucalypts
Low shrublands	0.46M km^2	saltbushes and bluebushes
Open forests	0.40M km^2	various eucalypts
Open herblands	0.12M km^2	Mitchell grass
Open heaths	0.11M km^2	numerous plants
Rainforests	0.07M km^2	numerous types
Unvegetated areas	0.05M km^2	saltlakes, tidal flats etc.
Seagrass meadows	0.05M km^2	seagrasses
Beach dune formations	0.03M km^2	various types
Salt marshes	0.01M km^2	various types
Mangroves	0.01M km^2	mangroves

Table 7.1 represents the different types of vegetation formations that existed before European settlement in 1788: the figures are approximate. Prior to European occupation most vegetation formations were modified by Aboriginal 'firestick farming' practices, and of course this pattern of land management would have continued in the early years of occupation in areas where Aborigines still had control over their land.

Formations most affected by European occupation—those being cleared for agriculture, grazing, mining, forestry and urbanisation—include woodlands, open scrubs, open forests and rainforests. Most other formations have either been partially cleared or otherwise altered by grazing stock.

Closed forests

Traditionally called jungles, closed forests are normally known as rainforests or, in some places, as scrubs. Such forests are found in the well-watered parts of eastern coastal Australia, Tasmania and in some isolated pockets along the northern coastline. The many different types of closed forest range from tropical rainforests such as those in the Wet Tropics region of far north Queensland to cool temperate rainforests found in Tasmania and on the higher coastal ranges of south-east Australia. Elsewhere there are the so-called dry rainforests, found mostly in drier and more inland localities; there are monsoonal rainforests, too, which occupy small niches around the billabongs or within the gorges of northernmost Australia. All but the cool temperate rainforests generally have a rich assemblage of plant life. Rainforests are not fire tolerant.

Open forests

Open forests are located in the moist, coastal districts ranging, with minor exceptions, from The Kimberley in Western Australia, across northern Australia, right down the east coast and across the southern coast of Victoria, as well as in Tasmania, south-western Western Australia, and along parts of the Mt Lofty Ranges and southern Flinders Ranges in South Australia. Most open forests are dominated by eucalypts although acacias (especially brigalow), casuarinas, cypress pines and paperbarks also form open forests. It is the eucalypt open forests which are most familiar to the capital city dwellers, for each city has eucalypt open forests on its doorstep.

Two different types of eucalypt open forest can be readily distinguished. Tall open forests, sometimes referred to as wet sclerophyll forests, occupy moist gullies and southerly aspected hillslopes in moist habitats. They include Australia's tallest trees and many are harvested for timber and woodchips. The second type of forest is Australia's most common forest type and is also called 'open forest' or, sometimes, dry sclerophyll forest. This type of forest is distinguished by trees with a maximum height range of 10–30 m. The understorey of such forests is sometimes shrubby (such as the ones seen around Sydney, New South Wales), or grassy (common in Queensland).

Many of these eucalypt forests are referred to as old-growth forests—that is, they are ecologically mature and have been subjected to minimal disturbance. These forests have high conservation values as well as being particularly beautiful to behold.

Woodlands

Of all of Australia's treed formations, woodlands are the most common type. The many varieties that exist are categorised according to dominant species, dominant tree heights and types of understoreys, which may be grassy, shrubby, or with spinifex. Woodlands are generally located on the drier, interior side of the open forests, though in some localities they abut the coast. Like open forests, woodlands are dominated by eucalypts, acacias, casuarinas, cypress pines and paperbarks, with eucalypts and acacias being the most common; many other species are well-represented, too. The eucalypt woodlands with an understorey of grass—the so-called grassy or savanna woodlands—are the most common type, being prevalent throughout northern Australia and on the inland side of the Great Dividing Range, where they have been extensively cleared for grazing and cropping.

Scrubs and heaths

There are both open and closed scrubs and heaths. Closed scrubs (which should not be confused with rainforest scrubs) are distinguished by densely growing shrubs—typically tea-trees or paperbarks—occupying swampy areas or depressions behind coastal dunes.

Open and closed heaths are not widespread in Australia but, owing to their location, are familiar to many city and coastal dwellers. They occupy sandy soils in coastal areas or coastal headlands, as well as some sand plains and sandstone plateaus. Australian heaths are relatively dense, scratchy formations, often of great diversity, and they like a good bushfire from time to time. In fact, many heath-formation plants need fire to germinate. While heath formations without trees are generally uncommon, many eucalypt open forest and woodland formations have a shrubby understorey composed of heathy plants. The sandy soils of the dry regions of southern Australia abutting the semi-arid and arid areas support quite large tracts of open heaths—for instance, the Ninety-Mile Desert of South Australia and the Big Desert of Victoria.

Open scrubs are like the open forests of the shrub world and most of them are dominated by the mallee. A kind of eucalypt, the mallee is a multi-stemmed plant up to 8 m tall, and comes in two basic types: the bull mallee, which has just a few thick stems; the whipstick mallee, which has many slender stems. The understorey varies from grassy to shrubby. Open scrubs are mostly located in southern Australia: ranging from western Victoria to north-western Western Australia, lying on the coastal side of the semi-arid regions; with minor areas elsewhere, usually in cold climates or in areas of impoverished soils. Much of the Australian mallee country has now been cleared for agriculture.

Shrublands

In terms of the area occupied, shrublands are perhaps the most widespread of Australia's vegetation formations. Some shrublands are dominated by mallee eucalypts (being less dense than their open scrub counterparts) but most are dominated by acacias, mulga (*Acacia aneura*) being the commonest. Mulga shrublands are found throughout much of semi-arid inland Australia. While only relatively small areas have been cleared, these formations have been subjected to extensive grazing by sheep and cattle on vast outback stations. Many of Australia's sand dune deserts, too, support sparse tracts of open shrublands dominated by acacias.

Low shrublands are mostly dominated by short-stature shrubs (up to 2 m, and normally less than 1 m) such as saltbushes and bluebushes. They are widespread across semi-arid and arid southern Australia, forming vast, empty plains or shrub-steppes like the Nullarbor Plain or the Hay Plain in New South Wales. Most low shrublands are extensively grazed by sheep and have suffered serious depletion and erosion problems in the past.

Herblands

There are many types of closed herblands such as alpine herbfields (found near and above the treeline), tussock grasslands (found on basalt soils or in alpine areas), sedgelands (for instance, the button-grass plains of south-west Tasmania), and fernlands. However, closed herblands occupy only small areas.

> PROBABLY AUSTRALIA'S MOST COMMON EUCALYPT IS THE VARIABLE-BARKED BLOOD-WOOD (*EUCALYPTUS DICHROMOPHLOIA*). ITS RANGE COVERS MOST OF THE SEMI-ARID REGIONS OF NORTHERN AUSTRALIA.

There are also herblands, which are far more widespread and common than closed herblands—though mostly in inland semi-arid and arid Australia. Tussock grasslands dominated by Mitchell grass are the most common type of herbland, being found across parts of northern Australia and western Queensland. These Mitchell grass plains produce the 'big-sky country' which many Australians think is typical of the outback: it is, but only in some places. Vast horizons, mirages and shadowy jump-ups (low flat-top hills) typify this extensively grazed country.

Other herblands occupy the coastal plains of northern Australia producing distinctive formations but particular mention should be made of a unique Australian herb—the spiky grass commonly known as spinifex or porcupine grass. Spinifex rarely forms formations in its own right but as an understorey plant it occupies about one-fifth of the continent, mostly in the arid regions. Many of Australia's deserts, while not that dry by world standards, are deemed deserts because of the unpalatability of spinifex to grazing stock.

The figures given for species numbers in tables 7.2 and 7.3 are approximate. It should be noted, too, that the genus *Eucalyptus* has recently been broken up into a number of different genera.

Overall, there are an estimated 20,000 species of native plants in Australia. Of these, about 17 per cent are considered rare or threatened with extinction. Almost half of the native plants under threat are found in the south-western portion of Western Australia, the area of Australia most thoroughly cleared of native vegetation.

TABLE 7.2
SPECIES NUMBERS OF COMMON AUSTRALIAN WOODY PLANT TYPES

Acacia (wattles, mulga etc.)	700+
Eucalyptus (gum trees, mallees etc.)	440
Grevillea	250
Hakea	140
Melaleuca (paperbarks)	140
Eremophila (emu bushes)	90
Banksia	80
Casuarina and *Allocasuarina* (she-oaks)	40+
Cassia	40
Atriplex (saltbushes)	40
Maireana (bluebushes)	40
Terminalia (nutwoods)	30

TABLE 7.3
SPECIES NUMBERS OF COMMON AUSTRALIAN HERBAL AND OTHER PLANT TYPES

Liverworts	1000
Asteraceae (daisies)	800+
Poaceae (grasses)	700+
Orchidaceae (orchids)	600+
Mosses	600

THE TALLEST HEATH IN AUSTRALIA IS *RICHEA PANDANIFOLIA*, WHICH IS FOUND IN TASMANIA AND GROWS UP TO 9 M IN HEIGHT.

TABLE 7.4
SOME SLOW-GROWING PLANTS

Stromatolites, WA	50 mm per century
Waddywood (*Acacia peuce*), Qld–NT	150 mm per century
Grass tree (*Xanthorrhoea australis*), WA	250 mm per century
Grass tree (*Kingia australis*), WA	300 mm per century
Huon pine (*Lagarostrobos franklinii*), Tas.	1200 mm per century

Stromatolites are not strictly plants in the normal sense of the word but rather a type of blue-green algae known as cyanobacteria. Blue-green algae is the world's oldest known form of life, having existed on the planet for the last 3500 million years. Matted sheets of this algae trap sediments which slowly grow and build up into what are known as stromatolites. They exist in a few colonies around the world, the best examples being at Hamelin Pool, Shark Bay, Western Australia.

I cannot vouch for the reliability of the waddywood growth rate given in table 7.4, which is derived from one source. But waddywood seedlings grow much faster than this. Given that waddywood grows to a height of nearly 15 m, then at this growth-rate mature specimens would be about 10,000 years old, a very improbable age.

TABLE 7.5
AGE OF PLANTS

Huon pine (*Lagarostrobos franklinii*), Tas.	2500 years
Antarctic beech (*Nothofagus moorei*), NSW–Vic.–Tas.	2000 years
Pencil pines (*Athrotaxis cupressoides*), Tas.	2000 years
Cycads (various spp), various States/Territories	1500 years
Kauri pine (*Agathis robusta*), Qld	1100 years
Karri (*Eucalyptus diversicolor*), WA	1000 years
Grass tree (*Kingia australis*), WA	1000 years
River red gum (*Eucalyptus camaldulensis*), various States/Territories	1000 years
Jarrah (*Eucalyptus marginata*), WA	1000 years
Baobab (*Adansonia gibbosa*), WA–NT	1000 years
Tree ferns (*Cyathea/Dicksonia* spp), NSW–Vic.–Qld–Tas.	500 years

A zamia palm at Mt Tambourine, McPherson Range, Queensland, now destroyed, was once claimed to be over 1500 years old. It is sad to think that in 1997 the Department of Conservation and Land Management in Western Australia cut down a 1000-year-old karri in an area proposed for a national park. In August 1997 news reports mentioned that a 2000-year-old Huon pine, which was starting to lean over, was likely to be removed if it proved to be a threat to tourists!

CHANGES TO VEGETATION FORMATIONS

The most significant changes to Australia's natural vegetation formations—and, consequently, to the Australian countryside—have been caused by the deliberate clearing of the land by European occupiers for grazing, agriculture, mining and urbanisation, and by the intentional use of, or incidental damage produced by bushfires.

Fire in itself will not drastically alter the vegetation formations in the long term, where those formations have evolved with fire. In fact, many plants depend on occasional fires in order to regenerate. The problem is that changes in the intensity and frequency of fires does alter and damage formations, especially those ones not able to cope with fires (for instance, rainforests). The prevention of fire also changes formations, for in the absence of fire the growth of shrubs is promoted at the expense of grasses. The eucalypt woodlands dominated by bimble box within the sub-humid/semi-arid country of eastern Australia were once considered to be good grazing land by the early pioneers. The prodigious growth of shrubs in their understoreys has rendered many of these woodlands partly useless for such purposes, however, and the use of fire as a management tool could have assisted in keeping this country open.

For hundreds of generations Aborigines had engaged in what is known as 'firestick farming', which had kept the countryside open and clear. By firing the land they promoted the growth of grasses as well as flushing out game. Regulating their burning to small areas and firing only during the cool seasons, they avoided major conflagrations and produced a mosaic of recently burnt areas, regenerating areas, and unburnt areas. This diversity enabled both plant and animal species to survive.

The partial or wholesale land-clearing that took place following European occupation had a far more dramatic impact. Where the removal of most or all of the vegetation had taken place, it was only a generation or two before there was an increase in soil erosion caused by the soil's greater exposure to wind and water. Streams became cloudy with sediment and waterholes silted up.

Maintaining stands of vegetation is important in the control of soil erosion. In humid country the crowns of trees provide protection for the understorey, which in turn protects a ground layer of grasses, mosses and fallen leaves. This ground layer absorbs rainwater, releasing it gradually, and thus regulates surface runoff and stream flows, which mitigates the effects of flooding rains in extreme circumstances. In dry areas stands of vegetation maintain a good ground-surface mulch of humus as well as breaking the velocity of the wind, thereby minimising the effects of wind erosion and the desiccating effect of hot northerly winds.

On some cleared land salt has entered the upper levels of the soil. As trees were removed the water table rose, bringing with it salts deposited at deeper levels. Stands of trees can reduce this soil contamination by salt; by utilising the groundwater, the trees keep the water table below the root zone of grasses and shrubs. The net result of wholesale land clearances, then, was not only soil loss but also the loss of otherwise productive farmlands.

Stocking, too, has affected the countryside: the natural herbage has not only been replaced with exotic plants in the form of improved pastures but it has also been depleted by grazing and browsing. Furthermore, trampling and compaction of soil has occurred with the introduction of hard-hoofed animals. Not all these changes were intentional. For instance, the introduction of the rabbit, for hunting in the 1850s, has led to major changes in the Australian countryside, especially in the southern semi-arid and arid regions. Not content with replacing native animals such as the bilby, rabbits have severely depleted the vegetation of the rangelands, permanently altering the nature of the landscape.

The net result of all these impacts is that the countryside has significantly changed since European occupation, in many cases for the worse. Unfortunately, massive land clearances are still occurring in Australia. Between 1983 and 1993 half a million hectares per year were cleared in Queensland alone, which accounted for 60 per cent of Australia's total (this figure includes the clearance of shrubby regrowth on already cleared land). This clearance rate is the equivalent of 70 football fields per hour and gave Australia the dubious ranking of the eighth-worst land-clearing country in the world for this ten-year period. Fortunately, though, there is a growing awareness in the community that the land can be abused only for so long.

DISTINCTIVE AUSTRALIAN TREES AND SHRUBS

TABLE 7.6
AUSTRALIA'S TALLEST TREE SPECIES

SPECIES	DISTRIBUTION	MAX. HEIGHT
Mountain ash (*Eucalyptus regnans*)	Vic.–Tas.	100 m+
Alpine ash (*Eucalyptus delegatensis*)	NSW–Vic.–Tas.	90 m
Shining gum (*Eucalyptus nitens*)	NSW–Vic.	90 m
Messmate stringybark (*Eucalyptus obliqua*)	NSW–Vic.–Qld–SA–Tas.	90 m
Karri (*Eucalyptus diversicolor*)	WA	85 m
Flooded gum (*Eucalyptus grandis*)	NSW–Qld	75 m
Maidens gum (*Eucalyptus maidenii*)	NSW–Vic.	75 m
Red tingle (*Eucalyptus jacksoni*)	WA	70 m
Tallowwood (*Eucalyptus microcorys*)	NSW–Qld	70 m
Blackbutt (*Eucalyptus pilularis*)	NSW–Qld	70 m
Tasmanian blue gum (*Eucalyptus globulus*)	Vic.–Tas.	70 m
Red cedar (*Toona australis*)	NSW–Qld	70 m
Spotted gum (*Eucalyptus maculata*)	NSW–Qld	70 m
Sydney blue gum (*Eucalyptus saligna*)	NSW–Qld	65 m
Round-leaved gum (*Eucalyptus deanei*)	NSW–Qld	65 m
Mountain grey gum (*Eucalyptus cypellocarpa*)	NSW–Vic.	65 m
Hoop pine (*Araucaria cunninghamii*)	NSW–Qld	60 m
Norfolk Island pine (*Araucaria heterophylla*)	Norfolk Island	60 m

Table 7.6 shows the maximum representative heights for trees growing under ideal conditions. All the eucalypts are found in tall open forests (wet sclerophyll forests); the tallowwood and shining gum may be located on the edge of some rainforests while hoop pines and red cedars are found in rainforests.

By way of interest, the trees that grow at the highest altitude in Australia are snow gums (*Eucalyptus pauciflora*) found in the vicinity of the upper Snowy River–Mt Kosciuszko area, Snowy Mountains, New South Wales. At around 2000 m these attractive plants form a treeline between the sub-alpine and alpine zones. This treeline is at lower elevations in sub-alpine valleys, as well as in Victoria and Tasmania.

TABLE 7.7
SOME TALL AUSTRALIAN TREES

mountain ash felled near Healesville, Central Highlands, Vic.	132.6 m
Cornthwaite Tree—mountain ash cut down near Thorpdale, Gippsland, Vic.	114.3 m
Maydena Tree—mountain ash, Styx Valley, Tas.	99 m
Grandis Tree—flooded gum, near Bulahdelah, NSW	87 m
karri cut down near Pemberton, WA	87 m
karri, near Warren River, WA	84.7 m
The Big Tree—mountain ash, in the Cumberland Valley, Victorian Alps, Vic.	84 m
Noble Tree—white gum, near Styx River, east of Armidale, NSW	79.2 m
Bird Tree—blackbutt, inland from Kendall, NSW	69 m
Big Fella Gum Tree—flooded gum, inland from Kendall, NSW	67 m
Gloucester Tree—karri, near Pemberton, WA	60 m
Kalpowar Queen—hoop pine, near Monto, Qld	46 m

The figure in table 7.7 for the mountain ash felled near Healesville is unreliable and not officially recognised. Nonetheless, it was claimed that this tree was about 145 m high when the topmost branches and stump were added. The height given for the Maydena Tree is before a lightning strike lopped off its top: this tree is approximately 61 m to its first branch, with a girth of 12.8 m, and is an estimated 300–350 years old. The Grandis Tree's figure includes a dead branch at its top; its living section is 84.3 m tall.

The Big Tree, if in fact it is the same tree once known as the Cumberland Tree, has been measured at nearly 92 m tall, with a girth of 4.1 m measured about 3 m above the ground. Nearby there were once 25 other tall trees with an average height of 81 m. The Gloucester Tree was originally 76.2 m tall before a bushfire lookout was built near its top.

By way of contrast, the shortest plant would appear to be the duckweed *Wolffia angusta*, found in tropical Australia, which grows to a height of 0.6 mm!

Some famous Australian trees

- Cathedral Fig—a strangler fig (*Ficus destruens*) near Lake Tinaroo, Atherton Tableland, Queensland. A striking fig set deep within a rainforest.
- Curtain Fig—a banyan (*Ficus columnaris*) near Yungaburra, Atherton Tableland, Queensland. Aerial roots up to 18 m tall descend from its sloping trunk to form an impressive and photographic curtain.
- Cazneaux Tree—a river red gum (*Eucalyptus camaldulensis*) near Wilpena Pound, Flinders Ranges, South Australia. An impressive tree estimated to be over 300 years old; made famous by the Cazneaux photograph 'Spirit of Endurance'.
- Diamond Tree—a karri (*Eucalyptus diversicolor*), Manjimup district, WA. A former lookout tower standing on top of a 51 m karri tree.
- Dig Tree—a coolabah (*Eucalyptus microtheca*) at Cooper Creek, Queensland. The tree carved by members of the ill-fated Burke and Wills expedition.
- Explorers' Tree—a blackbutt (*Eucalyptus pilularis*), near Katoomba, Blue Mountains, New South Wales. The tree said to have been carved by Lawson; he, with Blaxland and Wentworth were supposedly the first Europeans to cross the Blue Mountains.
- Foundation Tree—a South Australian blue gum (*Eucalyptus leucoxylon*), Glenelg, Adelaide, South Australia. The tree beneath which the government of the Colony of South Australia was proclaimed.
- Four Aces—karris (*Eucalyptus diversicolor*), Manjimup district, WA. Four tall karri trees ranging in height from 67 m to 79 m, and standing in near-perfect symmetry.
- Giant Tingle Tree—a red tingle (*Eucalyptus jacksoni*) near Walpole, Western Australia. A giant tree with a girth of 25 m. This tree is regarded as being one of the 10 largest living things on the planet.
- Gloucester Tree—a karri (*Eucalyptus diversicolor*), Pemberton, Western Australia. A famous tourist tree, complete with its terrifying spiral ladder giving access to the bushfire lookout on its top.
- Grandis Tree—a flooded gum (*Eucalyptus grandis*) near Bulahdelah, New South Wales. A popular tourist attraction and the tallest tree in New South Wales.
- Gregory Tree—a baobab (*Adansonia gibbosa*), near Timber Creek, Victoria River District, Northern Territory. The tree marked by the explorer Gregory.
- Herbig Tree—a red gum (*Eucalyptus* sp), Springton, Mt Lofty Ranges, South Australia. The temporary home of the Herbig family (Friedrich and Caroline), who lived in its hollowed trunk for two years in the 1850s and had two of their many children there.

- King Jarrah Tree—a jarrah (*Eucalyptus marginata*), near Manjimup, WA. A superb specimen of a jarrah, said to be over 600 years old.
- Prison Tree—a baobab (*Adansonia gibbosa*), Derby, Western Australia. A large-girthed (over 16 m) and hollowed baobab used for holding up to 12 prisoners in days gone by. Another baobab prison tree in Western Australia is located on the King River near Wyndham; with a girth of 10 m, it accommodated up to 18 prisoners. According to one source, the King River tree is 4000 years old!
- Sturt Tree—a river red gum (*Eucalyptus camaldulensis*), Wentworth, New South Wales. The tree nearby where explorer Sturt weighed anchor in 1830 after the discovery of the junction of the Murray and Darling Rivers.
- Tree of Knowledge—a ghost gum (*Eucalyptus papuana*), Barcaldine, Queensland. The birthplace of the Australian Labor Party.
- Twin ghost gums—a pair of ghost gums (*Eucalyptus papuana*), west of Alice Springs, Northern Territory. These photographic trees in their MacDonnell Ranges setting are a popular tourist attraction.
- Twin kauris—kauri pines (*Agathis robusta*), at Lake Barrine, Atherton Tableland, Queensland. A pair of impressive native pines overlooking Lake Barrine.
- Wollemi Pines—(*Wollemia nobilis*), Wollemi National Park, Central Tablelands, New South Wales. Located within 150 km of Sydney, this recently discovered stand of tall pine trees is of a species previously known only in the fossil record. Its ancestors have survived for millions of years, and so its discovery has captured the world's imagination, being likened to that of finding a small dinosaur still alive.

The stumps of giant trees, after felling, were sometimes put to good use during the pioneering days. Near Neerim, Gippsland, Victoria, a hollow stump was used as a house; elsewhere in Gippsland one tree stump had a track passing through it. Another tree stump in the same district, with an internal diameter of nearly 8 m, was roofed and used over the years as a dairy, church, school and horse stables. It could accommodate 20 people.

THOUGH NOT A FAMOUS TREE, THE MONGARLOWE MALLEE (*EUCALYPTUS RECURVA*) IS PROBABLY AUSTRALIA'S MOST ENDANGERED PLANT, THERE BEING BARELY FIVE OR SIX LIVING SPECIMENS ANYWHERE IN EXISTENCE. THEY ARE FOUND NEAR MONGARLOWE, SOUTHERN TABLELANDS, NEW SOUTH WALES.

Aboriginal people used trees for shelter, too. North of Melrose, Flinders Ranges, South Australia, there are many tree shelters utilising hollows burnt out or enlarged by fires at the base of the trees' trunks.

The south-east and south-west corners of the continent are interesting places for rare and endangered eucalypts. Many different types are found there, occupying small niches in stands that can be measured in tens or hundreds of plants. Many are found in cold or exposed locations. Not only are some of them relics of past cooler climatic conditions but these plants may well become the dominant plants in future vegetation formations when the planet once again swings towards another ice age—a good reason for preserving our endangered species.

Other big trees

- Monkira Monster—a coolabah (*Eucalyptus microtheca*), Neurragully Waterhole, Channel Country, Queensland. With a foliage circumference of about 230 m, it may be Australia's most spreading tree. The tree is about 18 m high, has a girth of 14 m and branches reaching out about 36 m.
- Colindale Giant—a fig (*Ficus* sp), Colindale Station north of Hughenden, Queensland. Another large, spreading fig tree, it has a foliage circumference of about 115 m and a girth of 6.7 m, and is approximately 30 m high.
- Largest Baobab in Captivity—(*Adansonia gibbosa*), Wyndham, Western Australia. Its foliage circumference is not known; but, given its foliage diameter of 25 m, a rough circumference would be about 75 m.
- Abbot Street Giant Fig—(*Ficus infectoris*), Cairns, Queensland. This big tree, now removed, had a foliage circumference of about 52 m. It stood 21 m high and had a girth of 6.8 m.
- Pekina Creek River Red Gum—(*Eucalyptus camaldulensis*), Orroroo, South Australia. One does not normally associate big trees with South Australia but this river red gum does have a trunk diameter of 3 m and a foliage diameter of 20 m.
- unnamed small-leaved fig—(*Ficus eugenioides*), Chichester State Forest, Hunter Valley, New South Wales. This fig tree is 50 m tall with a crown diameter of 40 m.
- Some other big trees, typically red tingles (*Eucalyptus jacksoni*), grow in the Valley of the Giants near Walpole, Western Australia. This area features a tree-top walk that is 40 m high, and the Ancient Empire of tingle trees, which have girths of 16 m.

Some species of figs can generally be relied upon for producing wide-spreading trees. A large fig (*Ficus* sp) close to my home near Nowra, New South Wales, has a foliage circumference in excess of the Abbot Street Giant Fig mentioned above and, though not as tall, it does have one branch 1.88 m in circumference.

THE BAOBAB (*ADANSONIA GIBBOSA*) IS A TREE THAT CONSISTENTLY HAS A VERY LARGE GIRTH—UP TO 15.7 M HAS BEEN MEASURED. IT IS FOUND IN THE KIMBERLEY AND THE VICTORIA RIVER DISTRICT OF WESTERN AUSTRALIA AND THE NORTHERN TERRITORY.

PROBABLY THE MOST COMMON AUSTRALIAN WOODY PLANT IS THE MULGA SHRUB (*ACACIA ANEURA*). IT SOMETIMES TAKES A TREED FORM; FOUND IN A NUMBER OF VEGETATION FORMATIONS, ESPECIALLY SHRUBLANDS, IT COVERS AN ESTIMATED AREA OF ABOUT 2.5 MILLION KM².

TABLE 7.8
SOME TALL SHRUB SPECIES

River cooba (*Acacia stenophylla*), mainland	15 m
Yarran (*Acacia homalophylla*), NSW–Qld	12 m
Cooba (*Acacia salicina*), mainland	12 m
White mallee (*Eucalyptus dumosa*), NSW–Vic.–SA	12 m
Mulga (*Acacia aneura*), mainland except Vic.	10 m
Green mallee (*Eucalyptus viridis*), NSW–Vic.–Qld–SA	10 m

The figures in table 7.8 are maximum heights grown under ideal conditions. Shrubs that are as tall as this may take on a more treed form, though still displaying the appearance of a shrub, with many trunks and branches growing from a singular trunk near ground level.

While certainly not a shrub, a rough tree fern (*Cyathea australis*), located in the Mt Dromederry Forest Preserve, on the New South Wales south coast, has been measured at 9.5 m tall.

THE MOST WIDESPREAD EUCALYPT TREE IS THE RIVER RED GUM (*EUCALYPTUS CAMALDULENSIS*), FOUND FORMING RIVERINE FORESTS AND WOODLANDS IN ALL MAINLAND AUSTRALIAN STATES/TERRITORIES.

EIGHT

THE SKY

The major feature of Australian skies is the weather. The weather is the state of the atmosphere at any point in time as determined by temperature, atmospheric pressure, humidity, wind speed and direction, degree of cloudiness, and so on. Collectively, when taken together and averaged out over many years, these conditions are described as climate.

The weather is a major controlling factor on the nature and appearance of the Australian countryside. In the long term it is responsible for the wearing down of the earth's surface—the erosion, transportation and deposition of soil and rock particles which contribute to producing the different landforms within the landscape. The major influences involved are wind, and water from precipitation—precipitation being any moisture that falls from the sky, in the form of rain, snow, sleet or hail.

The weather also exerts an influence on plant and animal life. The variations in temperature, precipitation, humidity and wind all combine with the soil and rock types to produce formations of vegetation which characterise particular tracts of countryside at any point in time. Long-term changes in weather—in other words, climatic change—will result in long-term changes to these characteristic formations, which of course will have an impact on the fauna whose survival depends on specific plants or vegetation formations.

Australian weather is generally characterised by fine and sunny conditions over much of the country for most of the time (see table 8.1). The area in Australia which has the least sunshine is the south-western region of Tasmania, with a yearly average of 4.8 hours per day. The sunniest areas, with a yearly average of 9.6 hours per day, are the north-west of Western Australia, and the eastern and northern parts of Central Australia, Northern Territory.

Nonetheless, despite the overall reasonably stable patterns of weather, variations do occur in the state of the skies and it is these that have the greatest impact on the Australian environment—producing events such as bushfires, floods, droughts and storms.

TABLE 8.1
AVERAGE DAILY SUNSHINE IN THE CAPITAL CITIES
AVERAGE NUMBER OF HOURS OF SUN PER DAY

	over the year	*in january*	*in June*
Sydney	6.7 hrs	7.2 hrs	5.2 hrs
Melbourne	5.7 hrs	8.1 hrs	3.4 hrs
Brisbane	7.5 hrs	7.5 hrs	6.6 hrs
Adelaide	6.9 hrs	9.9 hrs	4.2 hrs
Perth	7.9 hrs	10.1 hrs	4.8 hrs
Hobart	5.9 hrs	7.9 hrs	3.9 hrs
Darwin	8.5 hrs	5.9 hrs	9.7 hrs
Canberra	7.2 hrs	8.9 hrs	4.8 hrs

TABLE 8.2
RAINY DAYS AND CLEAR DAYS IN THE CAPITAL CITIES
AVERAGE NUMBER OF DAYS PER YEAR

	rainy days	*clear days*
Sydney	148	85
Melbourne	143	48
Brisbane	123	98
Adelaide	120	83
Perth	120	108
Hobart	162	22
Darwin	97	121
Canberra	110	83

Clear days are days virtually free of cloud. Note in table 8.2 that Sydney has more rainy days than Melbourne on average and that Hobart has the most number of rainy days of all the capitals. Perth is the wettest capital over the winter months.

The reason that Melbourne seems to be a rainier place than Sydney, even though it has barely more than half the average annual rainfall, is that much of Melbourne's rain falls as a steady drizzle over a period of days while Sydney's rain often falls as heavy but short showers. The rainier impression of a wet Melbourne is further enhanced by the relative consistency of its rainfall figures over a period of years (due in part to its southerly exposure to Bass Strait), while Sydney experiences a period of wetter years followed by a period of drier years (in part owing to the El Niño/La Niña effect).

Day-to-day weather changes

Day-to-day changes in weather are most apparent during calm conditions when the weather is under the influence of high pressure systems—the most noticeable feature being differing temperatures between day and night. The heat received by the earth from the sun during the day is lost during the night, with consequent cooler temperatures. If there is a protective blanket of cloud to intercept this outgoing radiation, this heat loss at night is reduced. Conversely, cloud cover during the day will intercept incoming heat from the sun, producing a lower temperature than would otherwise be expected if the skies were clear.

WYNDHAM, WESTERN AUSTRALIA, WHILE NOT NORMALLY CONSIDERED TO BE AUSTRALIA'S HOTTEST TOWN, DOES HAVE THE HIGHEST YEARLY AVERAGE TEMPERATURE BASED ON MAXIMUMS AND MINIMUMS.

Temperatures under these conditions are also affected by local winds, themselves formed in part by these day-to-day temperature differences. On-shore winds such as sea breezes lower temperatures, especially at times when oceanic waters are at their coolest. Conversely, temperatures may be raised by local winds blowing down the lee-side of mountain ranges.

Season-to-season weather changes

Seasonal variations are more complex and any understanding of why they occur involves looking at differences in air pressure (the highs and lows on the weather map) and the positions of these pressure systems over the country at different times of the year.

High and low pressure systems shift to the north during autumn and winter, and to the south during spring and summer. This shift follows, allowing for an appropriate time lag of about two months, the similar apparent movement of the sun. During the second half of the year the sun moves south and then, on the day of the summer solstice (20–22 December, depending on the number of years before or after the leap year adjustment), centres itself over the Tropic of Capricorn. Afterwards, it appears to head north, arriving over the Tropic of Cancer on the day of Australia's (that is, the southern hemisphere's) winter solstice (20–22 June). Then the sun again heads south. The earth's atmospheric pressure systems follow the same pattern of north and south movement.

From around November to April, the 'summer half' of the year, high pressure systems move across Australia from west to east along the southern fringes of the continent. These high pressure systems direct easterly winds over much of the land. Usually fine weather is experienced at this time. As the high pressure system passes, the winds tend to become north-westerly, directing warm to hot air onto the southern regions. If the high is slow-moving or becomes stationary the prevailing winds, again north-westerly, bring heatwave conditions to southern Australia. Extreme maximum temperatures have been recorded at this time. In the far north of the country moist air moves in from the equatorial regions bringing monsoonal (wet season) conditions.

Between May and October, the 'winter half' of the year, the high pressure systems still pass over the continent but take a more northerly path across the interior. Often they remain stationary for several days, bringing superb, sunny days followed by cool, even frosty nights. At this time northern Australia experiences dry and mild south-easterly winds (its dry season) while southern Australia is exposed to westerly winds and cold fronts associated with the low pressure systems that lie to the south of the high pressure belt. These fronts produce rainy and showery periods in southern Australia, though the south-east coast is often protected by the Great Dividing Range so that the days there tend to be cool but mostly sunny. If streams of cold air associated with these low pressure systems are directed onto the land, then cold, rainy or icy and snowy conditions will be experienced, especially in south-east Australia. These are the cold snaps of winter.

For a variety of reasons, which are only beginning to be understood, these seasonal variations do not behave the same way every year. During the winter of 1982 the high pressure systems—instead of centring themselves around 28°S latitude during late August, which is what might be expected—centred themselves around 34°S. This is where one would expect to find them during mid to late spring or mid autumn. As a result the weather experienced was more typical of spring or autumn than of winter. In eastern Australia that year the westerlies and cold fronts were limited to Tasmania and southernmost Victoria. This meant that a considerable part of New South Wales, northern and western Victoria and South Australia received little or no winter rainfall: drought, consequently, was declared over those parts of the country. This effect was repeated in 1994. It is now understood that El Niño—a term for the change in oceanic conditions in the Pacific Ocean—affects the pressure system patterns and, consequently, the weather experienced across the eastern half of Australia. An El Niño brings about below-average levels of rainfall. Its converse, La Niña, results in eastern Australia having higher than average rains, often for lengthy periods at a time. Significant La Niña conditions led to the flooding rains that inundated Charleville and Nyngan in 1990.

Extremes of temperature

Many regions in western New South Wales have recorded extreme maximums over 50°C. Such temperatures occur there primarily owing to the long trajectory of hot air emanating from Central Australia.

In 1845 near Strzelecki Creek, South Australia, the explorer Sturt recorded in his diaries an unofficial temperature of 55.6°C in the shade, and 69.4°C in the sun. An unofficial temperature of 53°C has been recorded at Cocklebiddy on the Nullarbor Plain, Western Australia.

TABLE 8.3
HIGHEST RECORDED TEMPERATURE FOR EACH STATE/TERRITORY

NSW	52.8°C	Bourke	17 January 1877
Vic.	50.8°C	Mildura	6 January 1906
Qld	53.1°C	Cloncurry	16 January 1889
SA	50.7°C	Oodnadatta	2 January 1960
WA	50.7°C	Eucla	22 January 1906
Tas.	40.9°C	Bushy Park	26 December 1945
NT	48.2°C	Charlotte Waters	2 January 1960
ACT	42.2°C	Canberra	11 January 1939
OSA	34.5°C	Cocos Islands, Indian Ocean	n.a.

TABLE 8.4
HIGHEST RECORDED TEMPERATURES IN THE CAPITAL CITIES

Sydney	45.3°C	14 January 1939
Melbourne	45.6°C	13 January 1939
Brisbane	43.2°C	26 January 1940
Adelaide	47.6°C	12 January 1939
Perth	46.2°C	23 February 1991
Hobart	40.8°C	4 January 1976
Darwin	40.5°C	17 October 1892
Canberra	42.2°C	1 February 1968

Note in table 8.4 which capital has the lowest of the maximum temperatures—the tropical city of Darwin. Tropical regions, particularly those on the coast, are typically very warm to hot all year but it is in the southern regions that higher extremes are obtained, owing to the long trajectory of warm air reaching across Australia.

The effect of the summer heatwave in 1939, resulting in the Black Friday bushfires in Victoria, can be clearly seen with three State capitals recording their highest-ever temperatures over three successive days

TABLE 8.5
WARMEST NIGHTS IN THE CAPITAL CITIES

Sydney	30.1°C	9 January 1983
Melbourne	30.6°C	1 February 1902
Brisbane	26.6°C	27 December 1952
Adelaide	33.5°C	January 1982
Perth	30.0°C	1 January 1997
Hobart	22.8°C	27 January 1954
Darwin	29.3°C	1 January 1968
Canberra	26.2°C	22 February 1960

In table 8.5 the highest minimum temperatures are recorded between 9 a.m. of one day and 9 a.m. of the following day. Adelaide's hottest night occurred during an extended drought period when Adelaide had seven consecutive days of maximum temperatures in excess of 37.8°C (100°F).

In January 1982, near the end of a record-breaking drought, Melbourne experienced a night-time minimum temperature of 31°C at 5 a.m. At 6 a.m. the temperature was 32°C, the highest ever recorded there at that time. A cool change moved through the city about an hour later, reducing the temperature by 10°C and thereby robbing that day of the record. In January 1997 Melbourne recorded its second-warmest night on record: 30.3°C.

TABLE 8.6
LOCATIONS RECORDING THE HIGHEST YEARLY
AVERAGE TEMPERATURE IN EACH STATE/TERRITORY

NSW	Tibooburra	20.6°C
Vic.	Mildura	16.9°C
Qld	Normanton	27.4°C
SA	Moomba	21.8°C
WA	Wyndham	29.9°C
Tas.	Eddystone Point	13.3°C
NT	Jabiru	28.1°C
ACT	Duntroon	13.4°C
OSA	Cocos Islands, Indian Ocean	26.9°C

In 1946 Wyndham experienced maximum temperatures in excess of 32.2°C (90°F on the old scale) for 333 days in a row.

Marble Bar, Western Australia, is normally considered to be Australia's hottest town but it can only manage a yearly average temperature of 27.6°C. Even its annual average maximum temperature, 35.3°C, would still not make it Australia's hottest town (see comments beneath table 8.7): that honour goes to Wyndham again—36.2°C. This is only beaten by the locality of Camballin in The Kimberley, which has an average maximum of 36.3°C.

TABLE 8.7
HOTTEST LOCATION IN EACH STATE/TERRITORY DURING THE HOTTEST MONTH

		hottest month	average temperature	average maximum temperature
NSW	Tibooburra	January	29.1°C	35.9°C
Vic.	Mildura	January	24.3°C	32.0°C
Qld	Boulia	January	31.6°C	38.5°C
SA	Oodnadatta	January	30.3°C	37.4°C
WA	Nyang Station, south of Onslow	February	33.7°C	42.2°C
Tas.	Launceston	January	17.7°C	24.3°C
NT	Roper Bar	November	32.1°C	39.2°C
ACT	Uriarra Forestry Camp, Southern Tablelands	January	23.5°C	31.6°C
OSA	Willis Island, Coral Sea	January	28.0°C	30.4°C

Table 8.7 shows average figures based on maximums and minimums recorded during the hottest month of the year at each location.

Marble Bar, Western Australia, is normally considered to be Australia's hottest town and it certainly is during December, its hottest month of the year. Then, it records a December average of 33.5°C, and a December maximum average of 41.7°C. On average, 107 days per year will see a maximum temperature in excess of 40°C. Between 31 October 1923 and 7 April 1924 there were 113 consecutive days of temperatures over 38.4°C (100°F) in Marble Bar.

Around Nyang Station is one of the hottest areas in Australia during the hottest months. There they can expect maximum temperatures in excess of 44.4°C (112°F) during February and 45.8°C (114.4°F) in March on at least one day in seven.

As a comparison, the coldest place in Australia at this time of year is Mt Wellington, near Hobart, Tasmania, with an average temperature during January of 8.5°C and an average minimum of 4.3°C.

TABLE 8.8
LOWEST RECORDED TEMPERATURE FOR EACH STATE/TERRITORY

NSW	Charlottes Pass	-23.0°C	18 June 1994
Vic.	Mt Hotham	-12.8°C	30 July 1931
Qld	Stanthorpe	-11.0°C	4 July 1895
SA	Yongala	-8.2°C	20 July 1976
WA	Dwellingup	-7.0°C	12 July 1967
Tas.	Shannon, Butler Gorge, Tarraleah	-13.0°C	30 June 1983
NT	Alice Springs	-7.5°C	12 July 1976
ACT	Canberra	-10.0°C	11 July 1971
OSA	Heard Island	-11.0°C	n.a.

There seems to be some confusion over the lowest temperature in Western Australia: some sources mention the 12 July 1969 figure of -6.7°C recorded at Booylgoo Springs, Murchison Goldfields.

In the Australian Antarctic Territory the Australian coastal station of Casey has recorded a minimum temperature of -41°C.

TABLE 8.9
LOWEST RECORDED TEMPERATURES IN THE CAPITAL CITIES

Sydney	2.1°C	22 June 1932
Melbourne	-2.8°C	21 July 1969
Brisbane	2.3°C	12 July 1894 & 2 July 1896
Adelaide	0.0°C	24 July 1908
Perth	1.2°C	7 July 1916
Hobart	-2.8°C	25 June 1972
Darwin	10.4°C	29 July 1942
Canberra	-10.0°C	11 July 1971

WORTHY OF NOTE IS WHITE CLIFFS, NEW SOUTH WALES, WHICH HAS THE GREATEST TEMPERATURE RANGE RECORDED IN AUSTRALIA: WITH A MAXIMUM OF 50.2°C AND A MINIMUM OF -7°C, IT HAS A RANGE OF 57.2°C.

111

The figures in table 8.9 represent the lowest temperatures recorded at the main city weather stations; lower temperatures have been recorded in the suburbs. For instance: -4.6°C at Pennant Hills, Sydney; -5.0°C at Aspendale, Melbourne; -3.3°C at Sandgate, Brisbane; -3.0°C at Parafield, Adelaide; -1.6°C at Guildford, Perth; and -6.7°C at The Springs, Hobart.

TABLE 8.10

COLDEST DAYS IN THE CAPITAL CITIES

Sydney	7.7°C	n.a.
Melbourne	4.4°C	n.a.
Brisbane	10.2°C	12 August 1954
Adelaide	7.2°C	8 August 1936
Perth	8.8°C	26 June 1956
Hobart	0.9°C	18 September 1951
Darwin	18.6°C	14 July 1968
Canberra	5.2°C	25 June 1949

By way of comparison, and even though it is probably not an extreme lowest maximum, the coldest day anywhere in Australia that I have found so far is a maximum of -9°C at Shannon, Tasmania, on 29 July 1973. Shannon is situated on the Central Plateau, at 940 m above sea level. In New South Wales the old weather station at Spencers Creek, Snowy Mountains, recorded a maximum of -5.8°C on 21 August 1962.

TABLE 8.11

LOCATIONS RECORDING THE LOWEST YEARLY AVERAGE TEMPERATURE IN EACH STATE/TERRITORY

NSW	Crackenback, near Thredbo	4.2°C
Vic.	Mt Hotham, Victorian Alps	6.1°C
Qld	Applethorpe Research Station, near Stanthorpe	14.5°C
SA	Stirling, Mt Lofty Ranges	13.2°C
WA	Mettler, north-east of Albany	14.8°C
Tas.	Mt Wellington, near Hobart	4.2°C
NT	Kulgera, Central Australia	20.6°C
ACT	Gudgenby Station, south of Tharwa	9.5°C
OSA	Macquarie Island, Southern Ocean	4.6°C

The estimated yearly average temperatures on Heard Island, Southern Ocean, are lower than those in table 8.11. There, yearly average temperatures are estimated at about 1°C at sea level and about -6°C near the summit of Big Ben, the island's highest mountain. In Australian Antarctic Territory the Australian base Mawson has a yearly average temperature of -10.5°C while the Russian base Vostok has a yearly average temperature of approximately -50°C.

AUSTRALIA'S COLDEST TRUE TOWN (AS OPPOSED TO ALPINE RESORTS OR SETTLEMENTS) IS CABRAMURRA, SNOWY MOUNTAINS, NEW SOUTH WALES: ITS YEARLY AVERAGE TEMPERATURE IS 7.7°C.

The coldest town in Tasmania is Waratah, on the west coast, with a yearly average of 8.4°C. By comparison, the old and now totally abandoned mining town of Kiandra, Snowy Mountains, New South Wales, was once Australia's coldest town, with a yearly average of 6.0°C. The coldest true alpine village (as opposed to an alpine service area) is the winter-snowbound resort of Charlottes Pass, Snowy Mountains, New South Wales, which has a yearly average of 4.9°C.

TABLE 8.12
COLDEST LOCATION IN EACH STATE/TERRITORY DURING THE COLDEST MONTH

		coldest month	average temperature	average minimum temperature
NSW	Crackenback, near Thredbo	August	-2.6°C	-5.1°C
Vic.	Mt Hotham, Victorian Alps	July	-1.4°C	-3.7°C
Qld	Applethorpe Research Station, near Stanthorpe	July	7.4°C	1.4°C
SA	Yongala, near Peterborough	July	7.4°C	1.9°C
WA	Wandering, near Boddington	July	9.7°C	4.2°C
Tas.	Mt Wellington, near Hobart	July	0.0°C	-1.9°C
NT	Kulgera, Central Australia	July	10.9°C	3.4°C
ACT	Gudgenby Station, south of Tharwa	July	3.0°C	-4.7°C
OSA	Macquarie Island	July	3.0°C	1.4°C

Heard Island, Southern Ocean, between June and October has an average temperature of -2°C at sea level and an average minimum temperature of approximately -5°C. Mawson, Australian Antarctic Territory, has a July average of -17.8°C and a July average minimum of -20.4°C.

As a comparison, the hottest settlement in Australia during the coldest month is Oenpelli, Arnhem Land, Northern Territory, which has a July average temperature of 25°C, and a July average maximum temperature of 32°C.

TABLE 8.13
SOME COLD COASTAL TEMPERATURES

Lowest coastal temperatures		
—on the mainland	-3.9°C	Eyre, Nullarbor Plain, WA
—in the tropics	-0.8°C	Mackay, Qld
—in Tasmania	-4.4°C	Swansea
—among off-shore locations	-11.0°C	Heard Island, Southern Ocean

IMPACTS OF DRY WEATHER CONDITIONS

Bushfires

Extended periods of hot, dry weather or drought conditions dry out the land. The combination of dried-out vegetation with winds and continued low levels of humidity provides ideal conditions for bushfires. Bushfires are wild fires which burn in forests and shrublands; fires that burn in grasslands are called grass fires. A fire that is deliberately lit by authorities to burn up ground fuel (such as leaf litter, sticks, and so on) and maintained under some sort of control is a controlled burn. Such burns are carried out to reduce the fierceness of dry season bushfires, or as a means of combating major conflagrations where property or persons are at risk.

The worst type of fire is a crown forest fire—when the crowns of the trees are ablaze. Because the gasses released by the leaves are very volatile, the crown appears to explode. These exploding gases are propelled by the prevailing wind to such an extent that these fires, which can move at great speed (80 km/hr or more), are virtually impossible to stop. Accompanying them, there are spot fires. A spot fire is one that runs ahead of a crown fire, having been ignited by air-borne embers originating from the main fire. An especially violent crown fire is known as a blow-up fire. Crown fires devastate all in their path; they are the fires of the newspaper headlines and usually result in loss of life and significant property damage.

Bushfires are a natural phenomenon, being ignited by lightning, and some types of vegetation have adapted to the presence of fire as a part of their ecology. More commonly, though, fires are started by people. They have a major impact on the environment, especially in the short term. In Febuary 1967 the Hobart bushfires destroyed approximately 1450 structures and took 62 lives. In 1974 a fire burnt out an area in western New South Wales of approximately 5 million hectares, roughly equal to 6 per cent of the State. Victoria's Ash Wednesday bushfires, in February 1983, destroyed 2000 houses, took 75 lives and burnt 335,000 hectares of countryside.

By far the worst fires were those experienced in Victoria and New South Wales in 1939. In January of that year a blocking high brought heatwave conditions for a fortnight with inland temperatures up to 47.7°C. On 8 January 43 homes destroyed and 2 people died at Dromana, Victoria. On 10 January 100 homes were destroyed and 19 people died, including 12 at the Rubicon timber mill. On 12 January some Victorian settlements were completely isolated by fires while Adelaide recorded its extreme maximum temperature of 47.6°C. On 13 January (Black Friday) Melbourne recorded 45.6°C and wind gusts up to 110 km/hr were experienced elsewhere. As a result of these extreme conditions 1000 homes were burnt out, phone lines, bridges, railway lines and public utilities were destroyed, and 50 people died across the State. In addition, approximately 1.5 million hectares were burnt, representing 6.5 per cent of the State. On 14 January Sydney recorded its extreme maximum of 45.3°C; as well, 6 people died and 1 million hectares of countryside was burnt. The Royal Commissioner investigating the fires, Leonard E.B. Stretton, reported that 'those fires were lit by the hand of man'.

Droughts

A drought results from a lack of adequate rain or from an extended period of dry weather. During a drought streams stop flowing. Equally, the water transpired by plants or produced by evaporation from the soil is inadequate to sustain plants and animals: so, only the most drought-resistant plants can survive.

Droughts occur frequently in Australia and most native plant life is usually well-equipped to deal with them. Introduced crops and animals can be severely affected, though, leading to crop failures, minimal planting of new crops, and the demise of introduced stock. Consequently, droughts have the most impact in areas given over to cropping or intensive grazing. Drought-like conditions are common in some areas that have extended dry seasons, such as the monsoonal tropics (no rain for 7–8 months), or Mediterranean-type climates (Adelaide and Perth, which are virtually rain-free for 3–4 months over summer). Droughts are least common in areas of regular winter rainfall—for instance, southernmost Victoria and Tasmania.

The droughts considered here are those ones in which the variability of rainfall is such that rainfall is equal to, or above average in some years, while in others it is so below the average that there is insufficient water for crops, stock or native vegetation. In economic terms, over the last 130 years there have been at least nine major droughts which have affected large parts of Australia—their severity usually being determined by the activity carried on within the drought area.

When the rains do return after extended drought conditions, they are often ineffective. This is because the ground surface, being unprotected and so dry, forms a hard crust; the rain simply runs off, often resulting in soil erosion. Only moderate soaking rains can effectively break a drought. Sometimes a light fall of rain or drizzle will fall over drought-affected crop or pasture lands resulting in a greening of the landscape by small plants which are inadequate for pasture use. This is a so-called green drought.

TABLE 8.14
DRIEST LOCATION IN EACH STATE/TERRITORY

		average annual rainfall
NSW	Yandama Downs Station, near Tibooburra	150 mm
Vic.	Neds Corner, west of Mildura	246 mm
Qld	Roseberth Station, near Birdsville	142 mm
SA	Murnpeowie Station, north-east of Lyndhurst	128 mm
WA	Deakin Siding, Nullarbor Plain	174 mm
Tas.	Ross	457 mm
NT	Charlotte Waters	128 mm
ACT	Duntroon	534 mm

As with all statistics, nothing is straightforward. Oodnadatta, South Australia, is Australia's driest town receiving an average of 117 mm of rain per year. It has not been listed in table 8.14 because the figure for the nearby Oodnadatta Meteorological Office is 158 mm per year. Similarly, at Forrest, Nullarbor Plain, Western Australia, the railway station receives 156 mm per year, making it the driest locality; but the Meteorological Office, located only 1.5 km away, receives an average of 182 mm per year.

The driest locality in Australia over the period for which records have been kept is Mulka Bore, Sturts Stony Desert, South Australia. In the 30 years of records (recorded during the early 20th century) the average annual rainfall was 100 mm. It is rare that no rain falls in any one year at any one Australian locality. The only record I can find for nil rain is at Mylyie Station, Western Australia, in 1924, but this may be unreliable. The lowest rainfall on record for any one year is 10.9 mm recorded in 1889 at Mungeranie Bore, Sturts Stony Desert, South Australia.

TABLE 8.15
LOCATIONS WITH THE MOST AND LEAST RAINY DAYS IN EACH STATE/TERRITORY
AVERAGE NUMBER OF RAINY DAYS PER YEAR

	most	*least*
NEW SOUTH WALES		
Deer Vale, west of Dorrigo	157	
Yandama Downs Station, near Tibooburra		13
VICTORIA		
Weeaproinah, Otway Range	206	
Neds Corner, west of Mildura		39
QUEENSLAND		
Millaa Millaa	166	
Monkira Station, Channel Country		14
SOUTH AUSTRALIA		
Mt Gambier Aerodrome	184	
Murnpeowie Station, north-east of Lyndhurst		10
WESTERN AUSTRALIA		
Sunnywest Farm, near Pemberton	191	
Cunyu Outstation, Murchison Goldfields		16
TASMANIA		
Waratah	253	
Chain of Lagoons, near St Marys		66
NORTHERN TERRITORY		
Darwin Aerodrome	108	
Erldunda Station, south of Alice Springs		15
AUSTRALIAN CAPITAL TERRITORY		
Canberra Aerodrome	110	
Duntroon		81
OFF-SHORE AUSTRALIA		
Macquarie Island	310	
Willis Island		129

Rainy days are days when at least 0.1 mm of rain falls. In Queensland the number of rainy days at Bellenden Ker Top Station, probably exceeds the figure given in table 8.15. Nearby South Johnstone Experimental Station averages 178 rainy days per year while South Johnstone Post Office, 1.5 km away, averages only 139 rainy days per year. Note the contrast in the Tasmania figures: Waratah is exposed and sits in the mountains which intercept the wet westerlies while the relatively dry Chain of Lagoons lies in a rainshadow.

IMPACTS OF WET AND STORMY WEATHER CONDITIONS

Floods

A flood is the inundation of land by water. It is caused by the inflow of tides or by a stream or streams overflowing their banks. Stream floods are caused by a number of factors, the most important being a high intensity of rainfall falling into a catchment or drainage basin. High intensity rains may occur as a result of storms—thunderstorms or tropical cyclones or rain depressions (the disintegrated remains of cyclones). Some of the low pressure systems that cross southern Australia during winter are also capable of producing high intensity falls. In restricted high altitude localities snow melt in spring can produce floods, as well. The likelihood of flooding increases in eastern Australia during La Niña years (opposite of El Niño), when there is a combination of an unstable atmosphere and prolonged rains.

The likelihood of floods is further enhanced when runoff conditions within the catchment have been modified, especially by the wholesale clearance of native vegetation. The sudden and massive flooding of Charleville, Queensland, in 1990 would have been exacerbated by the widespread clearing of the Warrego and Nive river basins further upstream. Old-timers said they had never seen the river rise so fast. Other factors that act to exacerbate floods include infilling or draining of back swamps (which are natural flood mitigators), or when floodwaters meet high tides in estuaries, or storm surges (which are raised sea levels brought about by low atmospheric conditions, such as those found beneath tropical cyclones).

The amount of rain that has previously fallen and the degree of inundation that this has already caused are also critical factors. Owing to the behaviour of water flowing through catchments, when all flooded tributaries coalesce they produce one or more flood peaks. A flood peak can be likened to a long, low wave of water moving downstream and its height will determine how widespread the flood is and what damage might result.

A flash flood is a special type of flood, common in mountainous terrain and in hilly areas devoid of vegetation cover, such as in arid areas. It is also common in urban areas where many streams are channelled and most of the vegetation cover

VOSTOK, A RUSSIAN BASE LOCATED IN AUSTRALIAN ANTARCTIC TERRITORY, HAS RECORDED A TEMPERATURE OF -89.6°C—A WORLD RECORD MINIMUM.

has been replaced with impervious concrete, bitumen and buildings. Flash floods are dangerous, for the water rises very rapidly and the flood peak passes quickly. In 1986 Sydney experienced widespread flash floods in low-lying areas.

The impact of a flood can be beneficial, as it carries rich deposits onto floodplains, which results in good pastures in low-lying country. But floods can also be devastating, when rapidly rising rivers pass through low-lying towns, or the country remains inundated for very long periods, stranding and drowning stock.

TABLE 8.16
WETTEST LOCATION IN EACH STATE/TERRITORY

		average annual rainfall
NSW	Tomewin, near Murwillumbah	2015 mm
Vic.	Wyelangta, Otway Range	1952 mm
Qld	Bellenden Ker Top Station	8629 mm
SA	Stirling, Mt Lofty Ranges	1189 mm
WA	Sunnywest Farm, near Pemberton	1484 mm
Tas.	Lake Margaret, near Queenstown	3580 mm
NT	Darwin Aerodrome	1535 mm
ACT	Jervis Bay	1170 mm
OSA	Christmas Island	2518 mm

AUSTRALIA'S WETTEST TOWN IS TULLY, IN FAR NORTH QUEENSLAND; IT RECEIVES AN AVERAGE OF 4321 MM PER YEAR SPREAD OVER 154 RAIN DAYS.

It is possible that higher amounts than those given in table 8.16 fall on Mt Kosciuszko, New South Wales, and in The Kimberley, Western Australia. In 1979 Bellenden Ker Top Station received 11,251 mm of rain (approximately 443 inches on the old scale).

Babinda, in the same area of Queensland, is sometimes quoted as Australia's wettest town; its average is 4174 mm per year over 151 rain days.

The highest total falls of rain generally occur on mountain ranges which intersect prevailing moist air streams. This orographic uplift combined with a succession of particularly wet months produced these damp extremes in table 8.17. Note that about 10 per cent of Bellenden Ker Top Station's total fell in one day (see table 8.19) and nearly half in January of that year.

TABLE 8.17
LOCATIONS RECORDING THE HIGHEST ANNUAL RAINFALL IN EACH STATE/TERRITORY

NSW	Tallowwood Point, North Coast	4,540 mm	1950
Vic.	Falls Creek SEC, Victorian Alps	3,738 mm	1956
Qld	Bellenden Ker Top Station	11,251 mm	1979
SA	Aldgate, Mt Lofty Ranges	1,853 mm	1917
WA	Jarrahdale, Darling Range	2,169 mm	1917
Tas.	Lake Margaret, near Queenstown	4,504 mm	1948
NT	Elizabeth Downs Station, Top End	2,966 mm	1973

TABLE 8.18
AVERAGE ANNUAL RAINFALL IN THE CAPITAL CITIES

Sydney	1215 mm
Melbourne	661 mm
Brisbane	1157 mm
Adelaide	531 mm
Perth	879 mm
Hobart	633 mm
Darwin	1536 mm
Canberra	639 mm

Note the relatively low figure for Hobart in table 8.18. This is the result of Hobart's being in a rainshadow: the nearby bulk of Mt Wellington and the rugged mountains of southwest Tasmania intercept the prevailing moist westerly winds.

TABLE 8.19
HIGHEST RAINFALL IN ONE DAY, FOR EACH STATE/TERRITORY

NSW	Dorrigo	809 mm	21 February 1954
Vic.	Tanbryn	375 mm	22 March 1983
Qld	Bellenden Ker Top Station	1140 mm	4 January 1979
SA	Motpena Station, near Parachilna	273 mm	14 March 1989
WA	Whim Creek	747 mm	3 April 1898
Tas.	Cullenswood, near St Marys	352 mm	22 March 1974
NT	Roper Valley, Top End	545 mm	15 April 1963

The fall at Whim Creek, cited in table 8.19, was due to a tropical cyclone; the average amount of rain there is normally 340 mm per year.

Bellenden Ker Top Station has also recorded the highest monthly rainfall figure of 5387 mm, in January 1979. In March 1996 Cape Tribulation, Queensland, received 765 mm in 24 hours and 1230 mm over a week.

TABLE 8.20
HIGHEST RAINFALL IN ONE DAY, IN THE CAPITAL CITIES

Sydney	328 mm	5 August 1986
Melbourne	108 mm	29 January 1963
Brisbane	465 mm	21 January 1887
Adelaide	141 mm	7 February 1925
Perth	107 mm	8 February 1992
Hobart	156 mm	15 September 1957
Darwin	296 mm	7 January 1897
Canberra	126 mm	15 March 1989

The Sydney figure, in table 8.20, resulted in the famous Sydney floods, which caused chaos as many roads were subjected to flash flooding. Sydney has also recorded 97 mm in a one-hour period. In 1984, too, the Sydney suburb of Turramurra recorded 167 mm in a two-hour period. Brisbane has had dumped on it 144 mm over three hours and 182 mm in a six-hour period

The incidence of snow

Snow will fall in air temperatures up to 7°C but will usually melt at once; if the temperature is lower than 3°C it will lie on the ground. Where the average minimum temperature of the coldest month is lower than -3°C it will remain on the ground for extended periods. At temperatures between -3°C and 4°C the ground cover may be patchy.

The temperature of crusted snow—that which has been subjected to freezing—can be determined by the noise it emits when walked upon: at around 0°C it makes a deep crunch; at -5°C it emits a high squeak; at -15°C, a very high squeak.

The highest peaks of the Snowy Mountains, Victorian Alps and Tasmanian Highlands may receive snow at any time of the year. Regular snow patches may remain all year in the Mt Kosciuszko area, and have also been known to remain all year on the southern slopes of Mt Anne in south-west Tasmania. It used to be claimed that in winter Australia had more snow than Switzerland.

Accumulations of snow can produce avalanches—especially of hard-packed snow and ice, such as is found in cornices located on the highest of the snow-covered peaks. One of the biggest recorded avalanches occurred in the winter of 1981 on the upper slopes of Mt Townshend, Snowy Mountains, New South Wales. It swept into Lady Northcotes Canyon and into the treeline below, flattening many trees and temporarily damming the valley. The path of destruction was still visible two years later.

The greatest fall of snow recorded over a seven-day period was 1170 mm at Spencers Creek, Snowy Mountains, New South Wales, in May 1964.

TABLE 8.21
INCIDENCE OF SNOW: BY STATE/TERRITORY AND CAPITAL CITIES

NEW SOUTH WALES
—regular winter ground cover above 1400 m along the Great Dividing Range
—occasional falls on the lower hillslopes, particularly above 300 m
Sydney: snow recorded on 14 days out of 146 years in parts of the metropolitan area (though this probably includes soft hail, which can be mistaken for snow).

VICTORIA
—regular winter ground cover above 1400 m along the Great Dividing Range
—occasional falls on the lower hillslopes
—rare falls over many of the southern Victorian hills
Melbourne: occasional falls on hills within 35 km of the city.

QUEENSLAND
—occasional falls along the Great Dividing Range as far north as the Bunya Mountains
—snow has been recorded at Roma
—other mentions include unofficial recordings in the Central Highlands and one reference to a fall of snow at Mackay
Brisbane: 3 light falls recorded in the last 100 years.

SOUTH AUSTRALIA
—occasional falls on the highest peaks of the Mt Lofty Ranges and Flinders Ranges and in the Jamestown-Peterborough district
Adelaide: recorded on 120 days in 128 years at Mt Lofty summit.

WESTERN AUSTRALIA
—occasional falls on the summit of Bluff Knoll, Stirling Range
—rare falls along the Darling Range
—snow recorded as far north as Wongan Hills
Perth: unlikely.

TABLE 8.21
(continued)

TASMANIA
—regular winter ground cover above 1000 m
—regular and occasional falls at lower altitudes
Hobart: regular snowfalls on the slopes of Mt Wellington during winter; occasional falls in the city, especially in the more elevated suburbs.

NORTHERN TERRITORY
—snow reported at Uluru
Darwin: never.

AUSTRALIAN CAPITAL TERRITORY
—regular winter ground cover above 1400 m
—occasional falls on the lower hillslopes
Canberra: regular falls on the hills outside the city; occasional falls within the city.

OFF-SHORE AUSTRALIA
—regular snowfalls on Macquarie Island
—Heard Island is mostly ice-clad

Storms

Everyone is familiar with storms. Storms happen when the stable conditions of the atmosphere have been disturbed. Storms are manifested by very strong winds and usually accompanied by rain or snow, thunder and lightning, and hail. The damage caused by storms can be total.

The most common storm is the thunderstorm. It occurs most frequently in northern Australia—with up to 60 thunder days per year in the Darwin region of the Northern Territory, compared to a maximum of 20 thunder days per year in southern Australia.

A thunderstorm is formed when heated air rises rapidly in the atmosphere and the water vapour it contains condenses at high altitude into water and ice. This frozen water, unable to be held aloft, then falls and in the process creates a down-draft of air. As it nears the earth's surface, this down-draft spreads out horizontally, creating strong gusts called squalls. Each uplift and down-draft of air is called a cell, and a thunderstorm may contain many cells in a huge cloud called a cumulonimbus. Cells rarely last more than 20 minutes but new cells may replace old ones, so a storm can last some hours.

When many thunderstorms come together into a single, highly organised storm, this is called a super-thunderstorm. Such storms are much more destructive: they may last over 12 hours, producing widespread flooding rains, damaging hail and many squall lines.

Willy-willies are very destructive, tornado-like winds, and are related to thunderstorms. These winds are characterised by funnel-shaped masses of air and uplifted material rotating very fast around a central axis. Fortunately, they are short-lived and their paths across the ground are very narrow; usually less than 500 m wide. Consequently, in sparsely inhabited areas they may pass by unnoticed but in urban areas their destructive presence is very apparent. A willy-willy passing over water forms a waterspout. Willy-willies should not be confused with dust devils, which are commonly seen in dry country (even car parks) on hot summer days. These small, whirling vortexes of dust and other raised materials are relatively harmless.

On a much larger scale are the most devastating storms of all—the tropical cyclones. Particularly severe tropical cyclones, such as Cyclone Tracy, cause total destruction when passing over settled areas. These storms form, and blow in the tropics; some, however, drift south into temperate regions and disintegrate into rain depressions.

Tropical cyclones form during the 'summer half' of the year in tropical waters and are remarkable for their wind speeds. Once fully formed, a cyclone is characterised by a huge swirling mass of cloud which reaches 10 km in height and may spread nearly 300 km from its centre. This cloudmass rotates in a clockwise direction (in the southern hemisphere) and at its centre is the eye: a clear or partly cloudy region, 20–60 km across, with light winds and no rain. Within this cloudmass and rotating round the eye, there are hurricane force winds—usually over 120 km/hr, sometimes over 240 km/hr—coupled with intense and widespread, flooding rains.

Still larger than cyclones, although rarely as violent, are the storms of the temperate latitudes, the extra-tropical cyclones. These are associated with the cyclonic low-pressure systems (or depressions) which cross southern Australia during the 'winter half' of the year. If sufficiently intense, these storms produce widespread gale-force winds—the dreaded 'winter westerlies'—which are often accompanied by thunderstorms, lashing showery rains and, at altitude, sleet and snow. On the lee side of mountain ranges—typically the Great Dividing Range, which acts as a rainshadow—the winds are cold and dry. These windstorms can last for several days, with widespread damage resulting when the winds are exceptionally strong.

The 'westerlies'—which are, in fact, mostly south-westerlies and sometimes southerlies—are often preceded by vigorous north-westerlies blowing off the inland. These winds are usually dry and can reach gale force at times. Passing over drought-affected land, bare paddocks or arid areas, they raise dust, so producing dust storms. The immediate effects of dust storms include reduced visibility, a choking atmosphere, and the deposition of dust. In the main, dust storms are a consequence of non-Aboriginal occupation—of land clearances and overgrazing.

As a south-westerly approaches, there is a sudden change in wind direction, a drop in temperature, often squalls and occasionally thunderstorms. These sudden changes are called cold fronts or, if less intense, cool changes. These fronts and their preceding winds may also cause widespread damage, especially during late winter–early spring. Cool changes also herald the cool southerly winds of summer, some of which may be vigorous and storm-like. But not all changes are storm-like: in the stable atmosphere of late summer–autumn some changes are so weak they might pass through without notice.

Another type of storm, occasionally experienced on the east coast of Australia south of 25° of latitude, is known as the 'east coast low'. When easterly moving, upper-level, low pressure systems cross over the Great Dividing Range and pass over a warm body of oceanic water, an intense cyclonic depression—similar to a tropical cyclone—can form. Once underway, and if sufficiently intense, this depression directs continual heavy rain and high winds onto the coast, resulting in floods, storm surges and heavy seas. These lows are most common in the transition years between El Niño and La Niña events.

TABLE 8.22
WIND SPEEDS AND THE STRONGEST RECORDED WIND GUSTS IN THE CAPITAL CITIES

	average wind speed	strongest gust
Sydney	11.6 km/hr	153 km/hr
Melbourne	12.3 km/hr	119 km/hr
Brisbane	10.8 km/hr	128 km/hr
Adelaide	12.4 km/hr	148 km/hr
Perth	15.6 km/hr	156 km/hr
Hobart	11.5 km/hr	150 km/hr
Darwin	9.2 km/hr	217 km/hr
Canberra	5.8 km/hr	128 km/hr

The figure in table 8.22 for Darwin was recorded during Cyclone Tracy.

The greatest wind speeds recorded were 259 km/hr at Mardie Station in north-west Western Australia during Cyclone Trixie. One source refers to a wind speed of 280 km/hr during a cyclone at Borroloola, Northern Territory, but this figure is not reliable.

In January 1991 a tornado swept through upper North Shore suburbs in Sydney, during which wind speeds are estimated to have reached 290 km/hr. On 15 December 1967 a tornado cut a swathe of destruction through the Sydney suburb of Mosman. In some 90 seconds a funnel some 600 m high and 45 m wide extensively destroyed 250 buildings; wind speeds were estimated at 200 km/hr.

MAPS

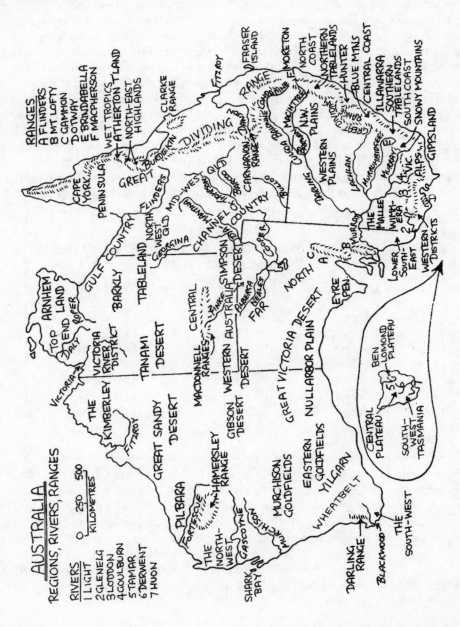

RANGES
A FLINDERS
B MT LOFTY
C GAMMON
D OTWAY
E BRINDABELLA
F MACPHERSON

FRASER ISLAND
MORETON
NORTH COAST
NORTHERN TABLELANDS
HUNTER
BLUE MTNS
CENTRAL COAST
ILLAWARRA
SOUTHERN
SOUTH COAST
SNOWY MOUNTAINS

GREAT DIVIDING RANGE

WET TROPICS
ATHERTON T'LAND
NORTH-EAST HIGHLANDS
CLARKE RANGE

CAPE YORK PENINSULA

BURDEKIN

FITZROY

MACINTYRE
GWYDIR
NAMOI
N.W. PLAINS
CASTLEREAGH
MACQUARIE
BOGAN
WESTERN PLAINS
LACHLAN

CARNARVON RANGE

FLINDERS
MID-WEST
QLD
NORTH WEST
TABLELAND
GEORGINA

CHANNEL COUNTRY
SIMPSON DESERT
COOPER

QLD

WARREGO
PAROO
DARLING
MURRUMBIDGEE
MURRAY
VIC.
THE MALLEE
WIMMERA
1. 2. 3. 4.
ALPS

GIPPSLAND

LOWER SOUTH-EAST

WESTERN DISTRICTS

GULF COUNTRY

ARNHEM LAND
TOP END
ROPER
DALY

BARKLY TABLELAND

CENTRAL
MACDONNELL RANGES
FINKE
ALBERGA
NEALES

FAR NORTH

NORTH C.
A.

EYRE PEN.

NULLARBOR PLAIN

BEN LOMOND PLATEAU

VICTORIA

THE KIMBERLEY

VICTORIA RIVER DISTRICT

TANAMI DESERT

GREAT SANDY DESERT

FITZROY

WESTERN AUSTRALIA
GIBSON DESERT

GREAT VICTORIA DESERT

CENTRAL PLATEAU
SOUTH-WEST TASMANIA

PILBARA

FORTESCUE
HAMERSLEY RANGE
THE NORTH-WEST

MURCHISON
GASCOYNE

MURCHISON GOLDFIELDS

EASTERN GOLDFIELDS
YILGARN

WHEATBELT

SHARK BAY

DARLING RANGE
BLACKWOOD
THE SOUTH-WEST

AUSTRALIA
REGIONS, RIVERS, RANGES

0 250 500
KILOMETRES

RIVERS
1 LIGHT
2 GLENELG
3 LODDON
4 GOULBURN
5 TAMAR
6 DERWENT
7 HUON

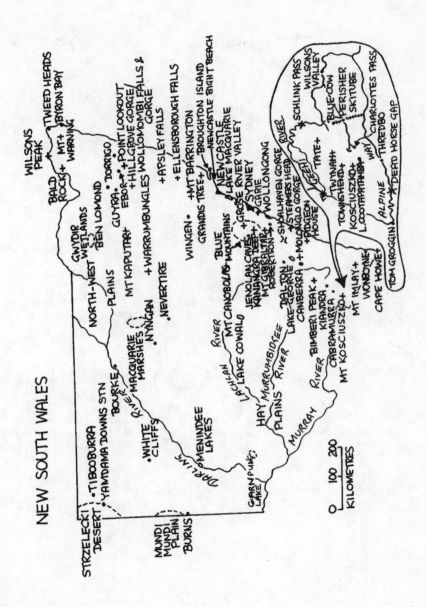

NEW SOUTH WALES

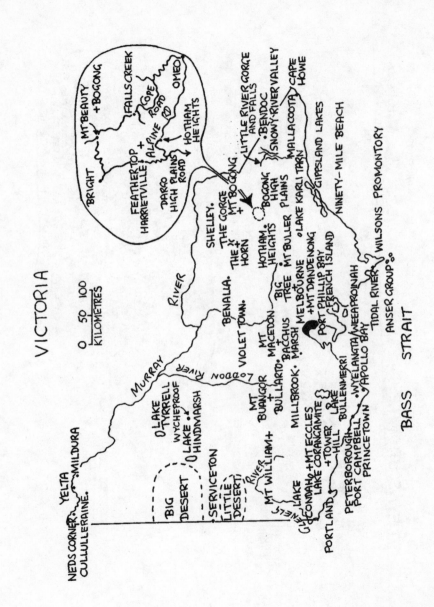

VICTORIA

0 50 100
KILOMETRES

MURRAY RIVER

LODDON RIVER

NEDS CORNER.
YELTA
.MILDURA
CULLULLERAINE.

O LAKE TYRELL
WYCHEPROOF.
O LAKE HINDMARSH

SERVICETON

BIG DESERT
LITTLE DESERT

GLENELG RIVER

MT WILLIAM+

MT BUANGOR+

BENALLA.

VIOLET TOWN.

MT MACEDON+
BULLARTO.
BACCHUS MARSH.

MILLBROOK.

LAKE CORANGAMITE
GLENONDAH+MT ECCLES
+TOWER HILL
LAKE BULLENMERRI

PORTLAND.

PETERBOROUGH.
PORT CAMPBELL
PRINCETOWN

WYELANGTA/ WEEAPROINAH
APOLLO BAY

SHELLEY.

THE GORGE
THE X+ HORN

HOTHAM. HEIGHTS
BIG TREE MT BULLER

MELBOURNE
+MT DANDENONG
PORT PHILLIP BAY
FRENCH ISLAND

MT BEAUTY
+BOGONG
FALLS CREEK
OPE
ALPINE ROAD
OMEO
FEATHERTOP+
HARRIETVILLE
BRIGHT
DARGO HIGH PLAINS ROAD
HOTHAM HEIGHTS

LITTLE RIVER GORGE AND FALLS
.BENDOC
SNOWY RIVER VALLEY

MT BOGONG+
BOGONG HIGH PLAINS

MALLACOOTA
CAPE HOWE

OLAKE KARL TARN
GIPPSLAND LAKES

NINETY-MILE BEACH

TIDAL RIVER
WILSONS PROMONTORY
ANSER GROUP

BASS STRAIT

BOIGU →•°SAIBAI BRAMBLE CAY
TORRES STRAIT
THURSDAY ISLAND
ENDEAVOUR STRAIT
CAPE YORK
SEISA
WET DESERT
QUEENSLAND

GORDONVALE
WALSHS PYRAMID
GILLES HIGHWAY
BELLENDEN KER
LAKE BARRINE
LAKE EACHAM
HERBERTON
THE CRATER
BARTLE FRERE
MILLAA MILLAA
TUMOULIN
RAVENSHOE
TULLY FALLS
PALMERSTON HWY

GULF OF CARPENTARIA

THE DESERT

MORNINGTON ISLAND

GULF TRACK

BURKETOWN
NORMANTON

BARRON FALLS & GORGE
THORNTON PEAK
MT CARBINE
CAIRNS

WILLIS ISLAND

HERBERT RIVER GORGE
HINCHINBROOK ISLAND
MT BOWEN
WALLAMAN FALLS

UNDARA LAVA TUBES
THE LYND

TOWNSVILLE

FLINDERS River

BURDEKIN River

REEF

0 100 200 300
KILOMETRES

CAMOOWEAL
CLONCURRY
BARKLY TABLELAND

WHITSUNDAYS
MT DALRYMPLE
MACKAY

DONAHUE HWY
BOULIA

DESERT UPLANDS

BROAD SOUND
SHOALWATER BAY

LAKE PHILIPPI
LONGREACH
BARCALDINE

ROCKHAMPTON
HERVEY BAY

SIMPSON DESERT
MONKIRA STN
LAKE MACHATTIE
ROSEBERTH STN
BARCOO River
CARNARVON GORGE

SEVENTY-FIVE MILE BEACH
FRASER ISLAND

QAALINE

POEPPEL CORNER
STURTS STONY DESERT
LAKE YAMMA YAMMA
CHARLEVILLE
ROMA

GREAT SANDY STRAIT
GLASSHOUSE MOUNTAINS
NOOSA LAKES
MORETON ISLAND

COOPER CREEK

TOOWOOMBA
MURPHYS CREEK
BRISBANE
COOLANGATTA
POINT DANGER

STRZELECKI DESERT

STANTHORPE
WILSONS PEAK
WALLANGARRA

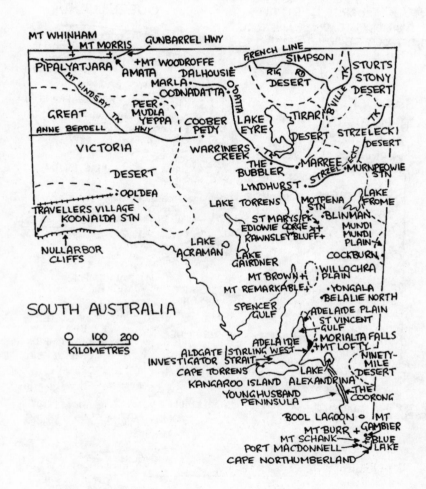

MT WHINHAM
MT MORRIS
GUNBARREL HWY
FRENCH LINE
SIMPSON
STURTS
STONY
DESERT
PIPALYATJARA
AMATA
+MT WOODROFFE
DALHOUSIE
RIG RD
DESERT
MARLA
OODNADATTA
MT LINDSAY TK
ODATTA
B'VILLE TK
TIRARI
PEER
MUDLA
YEPPA
HWY
COOBER
PEDY
LAKE
EYRE
DESERT
STRZELECKI
DESERT
GREAT
ANNE BEADELL
WARRINERS
CREEK
STRZELECKI TK
VICTORIA
THE
BUBBLER
MARREE
MURNPEOWIE
STN
DESERT
LYNDHURST
STREET
OOLDEA
LAKE TORRENS
MOTPENA
STN
LAKE
FROME
TRAVELLERS VILLAGE
KOONALDA STN
ST MARYS PK
EDIOWIE GORGE
RAWNSLEY BLUFF
BLINMAN
MUNDI
MUNDI
PLAIN
NULLARBOR
CLIFFS
LAKE
ACRAMAN
LAKE
GAIRDNER
COCKBURN
WILLOCHRA
PLAIN
MT BROWN +
MT REMARKABLE +
YONGALA
BELALIE NORTH
SOUTH AUSTRALIA
SPENCER
GULF
ADELAIDE PLAIN
ST VINCENT
GULF
MORIALTA FALLS
0 100 200
KILOMETRES
ALDGATE
INVESTIGATOR STRAIT
CAPE TORRENS
KANGAROO ISLAND
ADELAIDE
STIRLING WEST
+MT LOFTY
NINETY-
MILE
DESERT
LAKE
ALEXANDRINA
THE
COORONG
YOUNGHUSBAND
PENINSULA
BOOL LAGOON
MT
MT BURR +
GAMBIER
MT SCHANK
PORT MACDONNELL
BLUE
LAKE
CAPE NORTHUMBERLAND

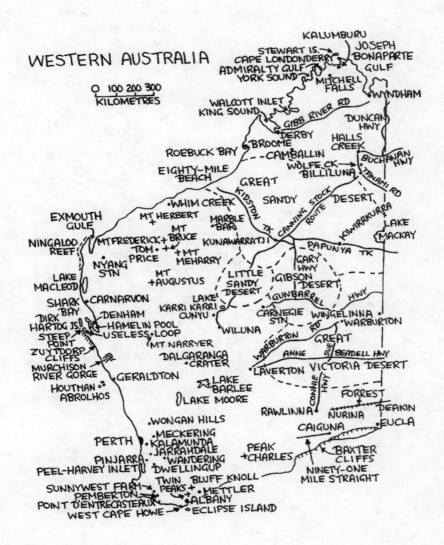

WESTERN AUSTRALIA

0 100 200 300
KILOMETRES

KALUMBURU
STEWART IS.
CAPE LONDONDERRY
JOSEPH
BONAPARTE
GULF
ADMIRALTY GULF
YORK SOUND
MITCHELL
FALLS
WYNDHAM
WALCOTT INLET
KING SOUND
GIBB RIVER RD
DUNCAN
HWY
DERBY
BROOME
HALLS
CREEK
ROEBUCK BAY
CAMBALLIN
BUCHANAN
HWY
EIGHTY-MILE
BEACH
WOLFE CK
BILLILUNA
TANAMI RD
GREAT
KIDSON TK
SANDY
CANNING STOCK ROUTE
DESERT
WHIM CREEK
MT HERBERT
KIWIRRKURRA
LAKE
MACKAY
EXMOUTH
GULF
MARBLE
BAR
MT
BRUCE
NINGALOO
REEF
MT FREDERICK
TOM
PRICE
MT
MEHARRY
KUNAWARRATJI
PAPUNYA TK
GARY
HWY
NYANG
STN
MT
AUGUSTUS
LITTLE
SANDY
DESERT
GIBSON
DESERT
LAKE
MACLEOD
GUNBARREL HWY
SHARK
BAY
CARNARVON
LAKE
KARRI KARRI
CUNYU
CARNEGIE
STN
WINGELINNA
WARBURTON
DIRK
HARTOG IS
DENHAM
HAMELIN POOL
USELESS LOOP
WILUNA
WARBURTON RD
GREAT
STEEP
POINT
MT NARRYER
ANNE
BEADELL HWY
ZUYTDORP
CLIFFS
DALGARANGA
CRATER
LAVERTON
VICTORIA DESERT
MURCHISON
RIVER GORGE
GERALDTON
LAKE
BARLEE
CONNIE
HWY
FORREST
HOUTMAN
ABROLHOS
LAKE MOORE
RAWLINNA
NURINA
DEAKIN
EUCLA
WONGAN HILLS
MECKERING
CAIGUNA
PERTH
KALAMUNDA
JARRAHDALE
WANDERING
PEAK
CHARLES
BAXTER
CLIFFS
PINJARRA
PEEL-HARVEY INLET
DWELLINGUP
NINETY-ONE
MILE STRAIGHT
SUNNYWEST FARM
PEMBERTON
TWIN
PEAKS
BLUFF KNOLL
METTLER
POINT D'ENTRECASTEAUX
ALBANY
WEST CAPE HOWE
ECLIPSE ISLAND

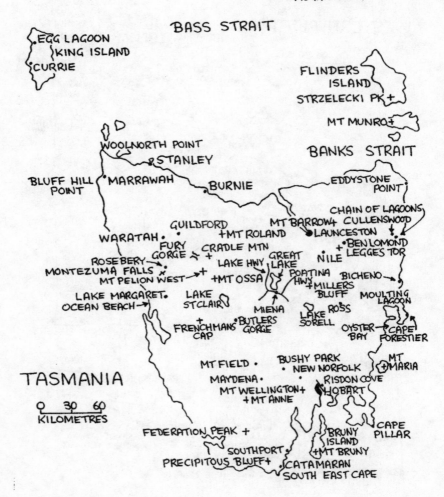

≈ HOGAN GROUP

BASS STRAIT

• EGG LAGOON
  • KING ISLAND
• CURRIE

FLINDERS
  ISLAND
STRZELECKI PK +

MT MUNRO +

WOOLNORTH POINT
  • STANLEY

BANKS STRAIT

BLUFF HILL
  POINT
        • MARRAWAH   • BURNIE

EDDYSTONE
  POINT

CHAIN OF LAGOONS
CULLENSWOOD

GUILDFORD
  • MT ROLAND
WARATAH •   + MT ROLAND   MT BARROW +
                                  • LAUNCESTON

FURY   CRADLE MTN
GORGE ×   +
ROSEBERY •   LAKE HWY GREAT
MONTEZUMA FALLS ×   LAKE
        MT PELION WEST → +
                      + MT OSSA   POATINA
LAKE MARGARET •   HWY
OCEAN BEACH →   LAKE   +MILLERS
                  ST CLAIR   BLUFF
            LAKE   LAKE
            ST CLAIR   SORELL   ROSS
        + FRENCHMANS • BUTLERS
          CAP   GORGE

+ BEN LOMOND
  LEGGES TOR

NILE

BICHENO →

MOULTING
  LAGOON

OYSTER + CAPE
  BAY   FORESTIER

MIENA •

MT FIELD •   BUSHY PARK
            • NEW NORFOLK
MAYDENA •   RISDON COVE
MT WELLINGTON +   • HOBART
    + MT ANNE

MT
+ MARIA

TASMANIA

0   30   60
KILOMETRES

FEDERATION PEAK +

CAPE
  PILLAR
BRUNY
  ISLAND
  + MT BRUNY
SOUTHPORT •
PRECIPITOUS BLUFF + • CATAMARAN
              SOUTH EAST CAPE

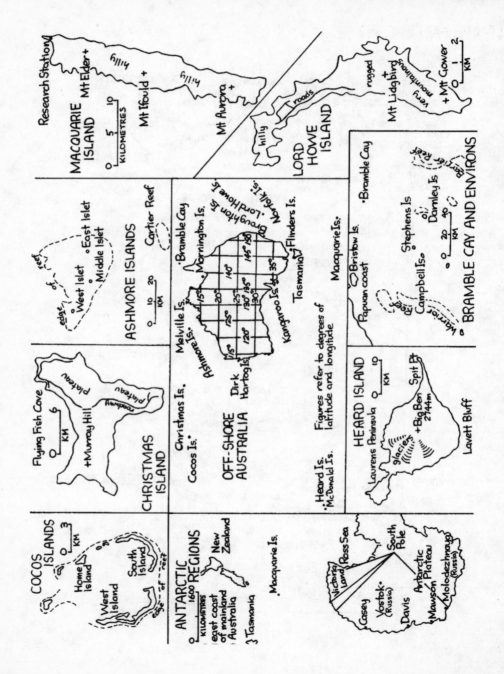

MACQUARIE ISLAND

Research Station
Mt Elder +
hilly
Mt Ifould +
hilly
Mt Aurora +

0 5 10
KILOMETRES

LORD HOWE ISLAND

hilly
roads
very mountainous
rugged
Mt Lidgbird +
+ Mt Gower

0 1 2
KM

ASHMORE ISLANDS

edge of reef
West Islet
East Islet
o Middle Islet
Cartier Reef

0 10 20
KM

OFF-SHORE AUSTRALIA

Bramble Cay
Melville Is.
Mornington Is.
Broughton Is.
Norfolk Is.
Lord Howe Is.
Ashmore Is.
115°
20°
25°
30°
140°
145° 150°
Dirk Hartog Is.
75°
125°
130° 135°
Kangaroo Is.
35°
Flinders I.
Tasmania
Macquarie Is.

Figures refer to degrees of latitude and longitude

Christmas Is.
Cocos Is.

Heard Is.
McDonald Is.

BRAMBLE CAY AND ENVIRONS

Bramble Cay
Barrier Reef
Stephens Is.
Darnley Is.
Bristow Is.
Papuan coast
Campbell Is.
Murray Is.

0 20 40
KM

CHRISTMAS ISLAND

Flying Fish Cove
roadway
Plateau
Plateau
+ Murray Hill

0 6
KM

HEARD ISLAND

Laurens Peninsula
+ Big Ben 2744m
Spit Pt
glacier
Lavett Bluff

0 10
KM

COCOS ISLANDS

Home Island
South Island
West Island
edge of reef

0 3
KM

ANTARCTIC REGIONS

New Zealand
Macquarie Is.
east coast of mainland Australia
Tasmania
South Pole
Ross Sea
Victoria Land
Casey
Vostok (Russia)
Davis
Antarctic Plateau
Mawson Plateau
Molodezhnaya (Russia)

0 1600
KILOMETRES

APPENDIX: UNUSUAL PLACENAMES

In the course of researching this book I came across a number of placenames that struck me as interesting, unusual or not particularly well-known. No doubt most were named by the earliest settlers and, while many would have fallen into disuse, it is interesting to contemplate how these names might have arisen. Some are self-explanatory, others are somewhat less obvious.

BLACKFELLOW BONES BORE	bore, north-east of Alice Springs, NT
BOY IN A BOAT	seasonal swamp, near Laverton, WA
CADIBARRAWIRRACANNA	salt lake, east of Coober Pedy, SA— *officially Australia's longest-named place*
CARDIVILLAWARRACURRACURRIEAPPARLANDOO	old name of a bore in SA, meaning 'reflection of the stars in the water'
COME-BY-CHANCE	small rural township, near Walgett, NSW
CROOKWELL	country town, Southern Tablelands, NSW
DEAD BULL CREEK, DEAD CALF CREEK, WILD COW CREEK	succession of creek names on the Bonang Highway, East Gippsland, Vic.
DEAD DOG FLAT	locality near Mt Garnet, Qld
EMOHRUO	homestead, in western NSW (say it backwards)
HOWLONG	country town, on the Murray River, NSW
LAKE MUCK	station, near the SA border in western NSW
LITTLE MOTHER OF DUCKS	small lake, near Guyra, New England, NSW
MUMMARRABOOGUNGOORANGIL	large swamp, near Duaringa, Fitzroy Basin, Qld
NO WHERE ELSE	old locality name near Sheffield, Tas.

SELDOM SEEN	mountain name and small roadhouse, at Wulgulmerang, East Gippsland, Vic.
TURN BACK JIMMY CREEK	creek, Riverina, NSW
UARDRY	siding on the old Hay railway line, Riverina, NSW
USELESS LOOP	salt-mining settlement, near Denham, WA
WAIT-A-WHILE	siding on the old Tocumwal railway line, Riverina, NSW
WILSONS DOWNFALL	settlement, near Tenterfield, Northern Tablelands, NSW
WING DING	station, in western NSW
YOULDOO	station, in western NSW
YOULTOO	station, near Youldoo

FURTHER READING

Australian Surveying and Land Information Group, 3rd series. 1980–1990. *Atlas of Australian Resources, Volumes One to Six*. AGPS, Canberra.

Barrett, C. 1944. *Australian Caves, Cliffs and Waterfalls*. Georgian House, Melbourne.

Bureau of Meteorology. 1977. *Manual of Meteorology*. AGPS, Canberra.

Clancy, R. 1995. *The Mapping of Terra Australis*. Universal Press, Sydney.

Commonwealth Year Book. various editions. AGPS, Canberra.

Cranby, S. 1993. *Oxford Australia Student Atlas*. OUP, Melbourne.

Groves, R.L. (ed.). 1981. *The Vegetation of Australia*. Cambridge University Press.

Elkin, A.P. 1980. *Aboriginal Men of High Degree*, UQP, Brisbane.

Fitzgerald, L. 1986. *Java La Grande: The Portuguese Discovery of Australia*. The Publishers, Hobart.

Flood, J. 1995. *Archaeology of the Dreamtime*. Angus and Robertson, Sydney.

Graetz, D., Fisher, R., Wilson, M. 1992. *Looking Back: The Changing Face of the Australian Continent, 1972–1992*. CSIRO, Canberra.

Halliday, I. & Hill, R. 1974. *A Field Guide to Australian Trees*. Rigby, Adelaide.

Jeans, D.N. (ed.). 1986. *Australia: A Geography, Volume One: The Natural Environment*. SUP, Sydney.

Johnson, K. 1992. *The Ausmap Atlas of Australia*. CUP, Melbourne.

Kirkpatrick, J.L. 1994. *A Continent Transformed: Human Impact on the Natural Vegetation of Australia*. OUP, Melbourne.

Laseron, C.F. (revised by J.N. Jennings). 1972. *The Face of Australia*. Angus and Robertson, Sydney.

Latz, P. 1995. *Bushfires and Bushtucker: Aboriginal Plant Use in Central Australia*. IAD Press, Alice Springs.

Lawrence, D.H. 1964. *Kangaroo*. William Heinemann Ltd, London.

Learmouth, N. & A. 1971. *Regional Landscapes of Australia*. Angus and Robertson, Sydney.

Leeper, G.W. (ed.). 1970. *The Australian Environment*. CSIRO, Sydney.

Peasley, W.J. 1983. *The Last of the Nomads*. Fremantle Arts Centre Press, Fremantle.

Ralph, B. 1996. *Longman Australian Atlas for Secondary Schools*. Addison, Wesley, Longman Australia, Melbourne.

Read, I.G. 1994. *The Bush: A Guide to the Vegetated Landscapes of Australia*. UNSW Press, Sydney.

Readers Digest. 1994. *Readers Digest Atlas of Australia*. Readers Digest (Australia), Sydney.

Recher, H.F. (ed.). 1976. *Scenic Wonders of Australia*. Readers Digest Services, Sydney.

Rodwell, P. (ed.). 1991. *Discover Australia*. Readers Digest, Sydney.

Sturman, A. & Tapper, N. 1996. *The Weather and Climate of Australia and New Zealand*. OUP, Melbourne.

Van Oosterzee, P. 1993. *The Centre: The Natural History of Australia's Desert Regions*. Reed, Sydney.

Year Book. various editions and various States/Territories.

INDEX

Page numbers in *italics* refer to table entries.